Evaluating Elections
A Handbook of Methods and Standards

In competitive and contested democratic elections, ensuring integrity is critical. *Evaluating Elections* shows why systematic analysis and reporting of election performance are important and how data-driven performance management can be used by election officials to improve elections. The authors outline how performance management systems can function in elections and their benefits for voters, candidates, and political parties. Journalists, election administrators, and even candidates all often ask whether recent elections were run well, whether there were problems in the administration of a particular state's elections, and how well elections were run across the country. The authors explain that such questions are difficult to answer because of the complexity of election administration and because there is currently no standard or accepted framework to assess the general quality of an election.

R. Michael Alvarez is professor of political science at the California Institute of Technology and codirector of the Caltech/MIT Voting Technology Project. Alvarez is a Fellow of the Political Methodology Society and is coeditor of the journal *Political Analysis*. He coauthored *Electronic Elections: The Perils and Promises of Digital Democracy* (with Thad E. Hall, 2010) and *Point, Click, and Vote: The Future of Internet Voting* (with Thad E. Hall, 2004).

Lonna Rae Atkeson is professor and Regents' Lecturer in the Political Science department at the University of New Mexico and director of the Center for the Study of Voting, Elections, and Democracy.

Thad E. Hall is associate professor of political science at the University of Utah. He coauthored *Electronic Elections: The Perils and Promises of Digital Democracy* (with R. Michael Alvarez, 2010) and *Point, Click, and Vote: The Future of Internet Voting* (with R. Michael Alvarez, 2004).

Evaluating Elections

A Handbook of Methods and Standards

R. MICHAEL ALVAREZ
California Institute of Technology

LONNA RAE ATKESON
University of New Mexico

THAD E. HALL
University of Utah

CAMBRIDGE UNIVERSITY PRESS
Cambridge, New York, Melbourne, Madrid, Cape Town,
Singapore, São Paulo, Delhi, Mexico City

Cambridge University Press
32 Avenue of the Americas, New York, NY 10013-2473, USA

www.cambridge.org
Information on this title: www.cambridge.org/9781107653054

First published 2013

Printed in the United States of America

A catalog record for this publication is available from the British Library.

Library of Congress Cataloging in Publication Data
Alvarez, R. Michael, 1964–
Evaluating elections : a handbook of methods and standards / R. Michael Alvarez,
Lonna Rae Atkeson, Thad Hall.
     p.   cm.
Includes bibliographical references and index.
ISBN 978-1-107-02762-6 (hardback) – ISBN 978-1-107-65305-4 (paperback)
1. Elections – United States – Handbooks, manuals, etc.   2. Elections – Handbooks,
manuals, etc.   I. Atkeson, Lonna Rae, 1965–   II. Hall, Thad E. (Thad Edward),
1968–   III. Title.
JK1976.A68   2012
324.6′5–DC23   2012014230

ISBN 978-1-107-02762-6 Hardback
ISBN 978-1-107-65305-4 Paperback

Contents

Contents   vii

Acknowledgments

This is a book that we have wanted to write for many years. We have each spent most of our professional lives trying to better understand how elections are conducted and how to improve the quality of elections. Throughout that time, we have learned a great deal from many people, who have given us the amazing opportunity to learn from their experience. Consequently, we have many organizations and people whom we wish to acknowledge.

Our work has been supported by many different organizations and institutions. Of course, we wish to thank our respective universities, the California Institute of Technology, the University of New Mexico, and the University of Utah, for their support of our efforts. In particular, we appreciate the staff assistance from Gloria Bain, Joann Buehler, and Cindy Brown. Financial support for the research we have conducted on election administration over the years has been provided by the Carnegie Corporation of New York, the John S. and James L. Knight Foundation, the John Randolph Haynes Foundation, the James Irvine Foundation, the JEFH Foundation, the JEHT Foundation, and the Pew Charitable Trusts. In particular, we wish to thank Ray Martinez III, Geri Mannion, Catherine Hazelton, Michael Caudell-Feagan, and David Becker.

We have each been lucky to have wonderful students with whom to work on projects like those that we discuss in this volume, both undergraduate and graduate. Their contributions, intellectual and personal, have made our research projects a great success. We thank Alex Adams,

David Barmore, Lisa Bryant, Nancy Carrillo, Peter Foley, Melanie
Goodrich, Erin Hartman, Gabriel Katz, Yann Kerevel, Ines Levin,
Morgan Llewellyn, Kathleen Moore, David Odegard, Erin Peterson,
Kim Proctor, Jon Rogoski, Steve Samford, Christopher Shannon, Andy
Sinclair, Betsy Sinclair, Lori Tafoya, Jessica Taverna, Lucy Williams,
and Luciana Zilberman.

Each of us has many colleagues to thank, and we appreciate
the help of Steve Allen, Steve Ansolabehere, Ernesto Calvo, Doug
Chapin, Marcelo Escolar, Ned Foley, Paul Gronke, Wendy Hansen,
Steve Huefner, Susan Hyde, Jeff Jonas, Jonathan Katz, Rod Kiewiet,
Tim Krebs, Robert Krimmer, Martha Kropf, Herb Lin, Cherie Maes-
tas, David Magleby, Chris Mann, Quin Monson, Robert Montjoy,
Jonathan Nagler, Grant Neeley, Jim Noel, Julia Pomares, Peter
Ordeshook, Steve Ott, Kelly Patterson, Ron Rapoport, Ron Rivest,
Mike Rocca, Gabe Sanchez, Kyle Saunders, Ted Selker, Philip Stark,
Bob Stein, Charles Stewart III, Walter Stone, Dan Tokaji, Caroline Tol-
bert, Alex Trechsel, William Winkler, and Rebecca Wright. In addition,
aspects of this book were presented at the 2008 American Political Science Association and at a talk given at IFES in 2008, and we thank
those who provided comments in those venues.

This work would not have been possible without close collaborations with election officials and policy makers throughout the world. In
particular, we wish to thank LuAnn Adams, Robert Adams, Pat Beck-
stead, Katie Blinn, Rhonda Burrows, Dana DeBeauvoir, Larry Del-
gado, Lynn Ellins, Efrain Escobedo, Valerie Espinoza, Dave Franks,
Ericka Haas, Shane Hamlin, Nick Handy, Fran Hanhardt, Governor Gary Herbert, Mary Herrera, Debbie Holmes, Neal Kelley, Scott
Konopasek, Denise Lamb, Patricia Lehmus, Tim Likness, John Lind-
back, Dean Logan, Epp Maaten, Ülle Madise, Connie McCormack,
Paul Miller, Rozan Mitchell, David Motz, Randy Newton, Maggie
Toulouse Oliver, Steve Rawlings, Governor Bill Richardson, Heiki
Sibul, Siiri Sillajõe, Sherrie Swensen, Mark Taylor, Rebecca Vigil-
Giron, and Kim Wyman.

We also wish to thank Robert Dreesen for his help making this book
a reality.

Finally, our hope is that the work that we have put into improving
elections will lead to a better democracy in the future for our children:
Ethan, William, Jackson, Carson, and Sophia. This book is dedicated
to that vision.

Introduction

Performance-Based Evaluation of Election Administration

There are a common set of questions journalists, election administrators, and candidates sometimes ask about the administration of elections in the United States and internationally. A reporter from a local newspaper will ask whether recent elections in the area were run well. During an interview with a national media outlet, one of us will be asked, in our roles as academics who study election administration, to opine about whether some state has recently done a good job administering a presidential, primary, or other federal, state, or local election. More broadly, we have been asked by journalists from other countries to evaluate how well elections across the United States have been run since the 2000 presidential election.

Although these questions may seem simple, they are inherently difficult and complicated because (1) election administration involves a complex set of procedures, (2) there are many possible aspects of an election to consider to determine if it was "run well," and (3) currently there is no accepted framework to assess the general quality of an election. More troubling, the question is focused solely on making a snap judgment about a given election – without taking the context of the election or the jurisdiction into account – and is not concerned with improving election management.

Over the past decade, we have worked with local election officials around the country and have found that most of them have a strong desire for well-run, glitch-free elections. They want a smooth voting day and want to know how they can improve their election processes.

They crave information that will help them meet these goals. Ironically, many election officials are unaware of the number of tools at their disposal to improve their election processes and procedures as well as the overall management of the process. They generate a great deal of data and could, with little cost, increase the amount of data and feedback and use that information to inform and improve their processes for the next election.

For example, in New Mexico, we have been working with election officials for some time, helping to collect information about their election processes: data on provisional balloting, overseas voting, poll worker training, voter attitudes and behavior, election observations, postelection audits, and so on. They have not only valuable information on the strengths and weaknesses within a particular election but also, more important, an ongoing examination and analysis of the election ecosystem that feeds back into the election administration processes and provides for reflection and improvement in the next election.

In Bernalillo County, Clerk Maggie Toulouse Oliver has found that consistent annual data collection and ecosystem evaluation efforts have provided her with valuable information and insight into what she and her staff are doing right, what processes and procedures are effective, and what needs to be done to improve the election experience for her county's voters and for her election. "Our goal is to always be working to improve the election process and the data and information we have received. Working with our academic counterparts has been invaluable to our efforts."

The systematic nature of the efforts in Bernalillo County allows officials to evaluate changes in performance over time and the way in which new processes and procedures either positively or negatively affect performance, for example, training of its poll workers. On the basis of performance-based evaluations initiated in the county, we determined using quantitative and qualitative observational data that there was an ongoing problem in the implementation of voter identification laws. Some poll workers asked for physical forms of identification, which was not in compliance with state laws.

On the basis of these initial findings, the state engaged in a voter education effort, producing a poster for each voting precinct on Election

Day that explained the voter identification laws in the state. Bernalillo County also changed its poll worker training on this issue and has continued to revise its training based on what has been learned after each election. By systematically conducting surveys and evaluations after each election, the county knows how well its poll workers are implementing the voter identification law, how well voters understand the law, and what needs to be changed for the next election.

Evaluating the election ecosystem may sound quite simple, but it is important to be systematic and detailed and engage in the data collection processes continually, election by election. Currently there is not a strong tradition of a data-driven evaluation of election administration in the United States, unlike public education, for example, where data are published annually to help the public, academics, policy makers, and administrators evaluate schools (test scores, dropout rates, per pupil spending, average class sizes, percentage of students on free and reduced lunch, and teacher qualifications). Such evaluation would include the following:

- Have elections been run with a high degree of integrity, free from fraud?
- How many people were turned away from the polls or voted provisionally?
- Are voters and stakeholders confident that ballots have been cast as intended and confident in the performance level of poll workers who run the elections?
- Did the poll workers report problems in the election?
- Are elections in the area convenient and accessible and do voters turn out to cast ballots in large numbers?
- Are there many reports of problems on Election Day in the area?
- Are election results reported in a timely manner, upheld by subsequent auditing procedures?
- Did the machines count the votes correctly?
- What was the roll-off on down ballot races?

Even if some of this information were available, it may not be clear from the data whether an election was well run. Again, without performance data, we have no standard for comparing elections, either historically or within or across jurisdictions.[1]

Performance Measurement in Government and the Private Sectors

There are six basic steps for developing performance-based management systems:

1. Determine the purpose of the performance measurement process.
2. Identify the organization's mission and customers being served.
3. Identify outcomes important to the organization.
4. Identify outcomes important to the customers of the service.
5. Select appropriate performance metrics that measure the outcomes.
6. Identify sources of data and how these data can be collected.

In the private sector, a performance-based management tool called Six Sigma has been designed to create a system within an organization that has 3.4 or fewer errors per one million events. The organization is constantly focused on ensuring that the process that takes the product or service from start to finish – from "concept to consumer" – is error free.[2] The central focus of Six Sigma is measuring performance constantly against an absolute benchmark and against previous performance. Collecting and analyzing data and involving individuals across the organization are core aspects of the Six Sigma process. The goal is

---

[1] This lack of data and performance analysis in elections is odd, especially considering what occurred in Florida in 2000 and because quality over time management-based data-driven evaluation processes are common in the private and public sectors. In the public sector, performance-based management is an integral part of federal, state, and local government budgeting, program management, and program planning in most jurisdictions (Moynihan 2008). In the private sector, it is very common for service and manufacturing sector firms to use customer surveys, market research, and data-driven methods to determine the quality of their services, products, and production processes. It is even becoming more common for colleges and universities to use data-driven quality performance evaluation, and these approaches are now becoming popular in primary and secondary public education throughout the United States.

[2] There are many hundreds of books and articles on Six Sigma. For an overview of the concept, see Truscott (2003). The preceding one-paragraph summary is only intended to explain aspects of Six Sigma, not the entire concept.

to use data so that the organization can know how good it is now, how good it can be, what are the barriers to getting better, and how can they be overcome. By establishing a process for improvement, these barriers and problems can be identified and improved.

Performance measurement is quite simple in concept, and variations of such systems have been used for more than a century. Frederick Taylor's scientific management and Edwards Deming's total quality management were precursors to today's performance-based management efforts. The two constants have been the collection of data – from the use of stopwatches to conduct time-and-motion studies to high-tech computer monitors in use in factories today – and the understanding that people operate within systems and that breakdowns in the system can hinder performance, even if individuals work hard and do the best that they can.

Management reforms of the past two decades have assumed that performance will improve when (1) managers have clear goals and results are measured against these goals, (2) managers have flexibility in resource use, (3) government decisions focus on outputs and outcomes rather than on inputs and procedures, and (4) managers are held accountable for the use of resources and the results produced.[3]

In the case of elections, it is possible to accomplish these four goals, but only if the election officials have thought about performance management at the outset. In elections, poll workers are only as good as their procedures and processes allow them to be. Elections have clear goals, clear sets of customers, and numerous opportunities for data collection and improvement. By having an array of data, across the full spectrum of election-related processes and activities, election officials can communicate effectively about what it is they do, what resources they need to get the job done, and how policy can be improved to make these activities and processes work better.

What underlies the importance of performance-based management is a very basic idea: it is almost impossible to have a discussion about what has happened, how effective a program is, how to improve a program, or how to make claims on additional governmental resources, without quality data (Kettl 1998). Managers can use these data both to improve their internal activities within the organization and to

---

[3] This list is taken almost verbatim from Moynihan (2006, 79).

strengthen the effectiveness of their collaborations with contractors and their communications with other policy players.[4]

Goals of Performance Measurement in Elections

In 2003, three Brookings Institution scholars noted that reforming government and government programs works "best when they [grow] from strong strategy and [have] robust intellectual support" (Dilulio et al. 1993, 9). The goal of this book is to provide a sound and strong strategy and provide intellectual support for reforming the management and operations of elections, both in the United States and internationally. Our focus is on how election officials can use data and performance measures to develop strategies for improving elections. Developing methodologies for collecting the necessary data, and approaches for analyzing them, is extremely important because without the systematic analysis of election data, election reform may be unresponsive to the needs of its clients and may be creating bureaucracies, administrative rules, and procedures as well as spending large sums of money on solutions for problems that do not exist.

What is a high-performance election? Local election officials will answer: "As long as we were not in the newspaper" or "As long as we don't get sued by a candidate." These are both reasonable answers; bad news stories or candidates suing election officials because of discrepancies in the implementation of election processes are clear signs of problems in the electoral machinery.

We want to think beyond the simplest definitions of a quality election and determine whether the various processes of the election were performed with high quality, regardless of whether the problems affected the election outcome or the experience of voters. Consider the following three examples:

1. A voter may be required to vote using a provisional ballot at a precinct because her name is not listed in the voter rolls and she thinks she is registered to vote there. She[5] may leave the precinct

---

[4] Addressing both internal organizational needs and external network needs is critical for effective government organizations. See, e.g., O'Toole and Meier (1999, 2003).

[5] Statistically, most voters are women, so we use feminine pronouns for ease of writing and because women are the modal gender in elections.

perfectly satisfied with her polling place experience and very confident that her ballot will be counted accurately. However, the voter does not know that the poll worker filled out the back of the provisional ballot incorrectly and that therefore her ballot will not be counted.

2. Voters who vote via absentee ballots in a jurisdiction may make more errors on their ballots – overvotes or undervotes – than voters voting in a precinct.

3. The voter registration file in a jurisdiction contains many voters who are no longer in the jurisdiction. This results in the misallocation of poll workers across precincts and the printing of too many ballots.

In many ways, elections are an activity where, from a management perspective, the inputs and outputs really matter. It is easy to forget that some elections, party primary elections, for example, are a government activity provided for the express benefit of third parties – the candidates and political parties who want to select candidates for their organization to run in the general election (which is why independent voters and voters who decline to state a party preference are often excluded from participating in primary elections). In all elections, candidates and parties are important customers of the election services and election officials should be (ideally) indifferent to the outcome. They should want their customers – the voters, candidates, and political parties – to be highly satisfied with the *process*, even if they are unhappy with the *actual outcome of the election* (in other words, they are confident in the process even if their favored candidate loses).

Elections Are about Data

Elections are about data, about counting votes and voters – and election administrators routinely engage in all sorts of procedures that generate vast quantities of information. However, much of these data are not generated for the purpose of evaluation. Instead, they are generated as part of the routine checks and redundancies of election administration. More troubling, these data are also often not combined with other data collected by the local election official (LEO) and used for performance-based management, organizational training, and quality improvement. Rarely are the detailed data from a postelection ballot audit provided to the public, or even to other election officials. When these data are reported to the public, it is usually in the form of an aggregated report such as overall results for a county or perhaps the results by precinct. The raw data describing the errors and source of errors are rarely included in these data reports.

We know of no jurisdictions where these results are reported in a way that makes it convenient or possible to compare the postelection audit results across counties or across states. The lack of reporting of detailed data from postelection ballot audits and the subsequent lack of analysis mean that valuable opportunities to study the performance of voting systems across jurisdictions, voting populations, voting technologies, and election administration procedures and practices are lost.

One example of data that could be invaluable for evaluating election performance and for performance-based management comes from the provisional voting process used throughout the United States. Provisional voting, often known more generally as failsafe voting, is a procedure intended to allow a potentially eligible voter to obtain and cast a ballot even if her name does not appear on the voting registry used in the polling place. Typically those who use the provisional voting process will mark their ballots, put their marked ballots into privacy sleeves, and then place the privacy sleeves containing their ballots into larger envelopes. On the exterior of this larger envelope are places for the potential voter to write her name and address, an affidavit for the voter to sign, and components that the poll worker must complete. Completed provisional ballots are then taken back to the elections office, where the information on the exterior envelope is compared to the complete and final voter registration database for that election. If the potential voter is found in the database, her ballot may be included in the tabulation, but if she is not found in the database, her ballot will not be included in the tabulation.[6]

---

[6] We say "may be included" as there are a variety of regulations that will govern whether the ballot, or some part of it, is eventually tabulated. For example, some jurisdictions require that the provisional ballot be cast from the voter's correct precinct – meaning that if a registered voter casts a provisional ballot from a precinct other than her own, it may not be tabulated. And in other places, if a voter marks a provisional ballot in the incorrect precinct, election officials will count only those races in which the voter was eligible to participate.

Another example of invaluable data is the number of provisional ballots completed and tabulated in an election. It might be seen as a potential measure of the quality of a jurisdiction's voter registration process. A voter whose name is not on the registry but who casts a valid ballot through the provisional process is a voter whose name should have appeared in the registry in the polling place. Information about the precincts where provisional ballots are most likely to be cast and about the demographic characteristics of provisional voters is critical for understanding the population of voters for whom the voter registration system is not performing adequately (Alvarez and Hall 2009; Atkeson et al. 2009). Moreover, because completing the provisional ballot requires the poll worker to complete certain tasks as well, the ability of poll workers to do these tasks correctly can be a measure of training effectiveness and poll worker competence.

Another example of underutilized performance data are those data generated in postelection ballot audits. Some states, like California, have long mandated that counties conduct routine postelection audits of ballots cast in elections, primarily as a simple means of verifying that the voting systems used in each county are tabulating votes as expected. Other states, like New Mexico, have recently implemented more complicated risk-limiting postelection ballot audits. In other parts of the world, nations employ independent auditing firms to conduct postelection audits.[7]

These postelection ballot audits collect an amazing array of valuable data. A typical postelection ballot audit has an election official select some random sampling of ballots or ballots from a sampling of precincts; the ballots included in the audit are recounted by hand, and those results are compared to the reported results from the initial tabulation. Discrepancies between the original results and the audited results in a single election jurisdiction can indicate malfunctioning voting systems or that the voters are not interacting correctly with the technology used to count their votes and that better voter ballot education is necessary.

---

[7] An excellent example of another nation that has employed independent auditors in past elections in Estonia. See Hall and Maaten (2008) for a discussion of this type of auditing.

Collection, Transparency, and Openness

A data-driven performance evaluation process for election administration will require federal, state, and local election officials to do two things. First, they must develop standardized election administration data metrics that are collected in an electronic format in a standardized manner. Across various states – and often across local election jurisdictions within a single state – various election data are collected differently and reported differently, and in very different formats (see Alvarez and Hall 2006; Kimball and Baybeck 2008). Some local governments do not collect data electronically or systematically organize and report data that they have on hand. Across states, there are different definitions for the same term – for example, voting in person before an election in some states is *early voting*, whereas in other states, it is *in-person absentee voting* – and these data on early or absentee voting may not be kept separate from data on Election Day voting. For example, data on uncounted votes in a given race may not be available for specific modes of voting, which means that it is not possible to identify problems that may exist with the voting process in absentee or Election Day voting.

Second, data-driven performance-based management in elections will require unprecedented levels of transparency on the part of state and local election officials. In many states, election laws explicitly do not provide local governments enough time or resources to capture data about the election before the election has to be certified and the data from the election sealed. For example, in Georgia, election officials have fewer than three days to certify an election because of the state law governing runoff elections. Once the election is certified, state law requires the election data – from counts of provisional ballots and problems that might have ensued to cause absentee ballot rejections – to be sealed and not be opened without a court order. For a data-driven performance-based management process to be put in place, state laws must facilitate the capture of data, and those who control the access to data must be willing to use those data, or to provide those data to others, to conduct evaluations.

Our collective experience suggests that most election administrators want to – and try to – conduct efficient and effective elections and engage in many activities to ensure a smooth election process. Over the past decade, transparency and openness have not always characterized election administration. It is often forgotten that although most voters in the United States live in large jurisdictions with more than 50,000 voters, most election jurisdictions are small counties with fewer than 2,000 voters (Kimball and Baybeck 2008). With few elections-focused staff and potentially few resources, these smaller jurisdictions often need assistance in developing the performance-based management systems necessary for a data-centered performance-based management process.

In other cases, election administrators may have made data available to the media, academics, or an interest group only to end up burned when the data were used in a way that they felt was incorrect or inappropriate. However, some election jurisdictions simply are unwilling to allow external scrutiny of how their elections are conducted. For them, performance-based management may be a threat to the get-along-go-along culture that exists in their election jurisdiction. Ironically, the best way for LEOs to deal with their critics would be to have data available to combat the anecdotal stories, usually based on a single occurrence, that litter the election landscape.

Since the 2000 election, the quality and availability of some data has improved. The Pew Charitable Trusts' Data for Democracy initiative,[8] the U.S. Election Assistance Commission's Election Day Surveys,[9] and the 2008 Survey of the Performance of American Elections[10] are examples of extensive data collection efforts where initiatives have been taken to collect important data from all states or from all jurisdictions within a state in standardized formats that were then made public in highly user-friendly formats.

However, data from the Election Day Surveys or the Performance of American Elections surveys provide only snapshots of certain aspects of elections. Election administration is a broad ecosystem, and it is critical to evaluate all aspects of that ecosystem. This requires examining data from (1) the process of the election (how many ballots went

---

[8] For information on Data for Democracy, see http://www.pewtrusts.org/our_work_report_detail.aspx?id=46594.

[9] For information on the EAC Election Day Surveys, see http://www.eac.gov/research/election_administration_and_voting_survey.aspx.

[10] For more information about the Survey of the Performance of American Elections, see http://vote.caltech.edu/drupal/node/231.

uncounted, what was the overall turnout rate in the election, or is the count accurate?), (2) the experience voters had with the election (did voters have problems at the polls and are they confident in the election process?), and (3) the experience poll workers had in the voting process (did they feel well trained and have any systematic problems administering the election?).

Consider the analogy between voting and Apple Computer. It is not enough for Apple that its manufacturing process goes well, with few defects in the manufacturing. For Apple, it is also important that its customers like its products (and yes, voting is a service product that government provides its citizens!) and that its Apple Store staff feel well trained to sell the products and services offered there. For Apple to know that all of these things are true, it has to look at data on manufacturing defects, product returns, product sales, customer complaints, employee feedback, and an array of related information. Election officials need the same array of metrics to engage in performance-based management efforts and for others to evaluate the performance of elections in their communities.

For performance evaluation and management process to take place, election officials will have to collect more data, more systematically, and then be much more open and transparent in sharing those data publicly than they typically have been in the past.

In the chapters that follow, we will make two different points time and again:

- First, we will articulate how election administrators can gain valuable feedback by employing the methods we present and use this information to implement performance-based management techniques that will improve election administration. If election administrators understand that they have a great deal to gain by studying their own performance, then they will want to adopt some or all of these evaluation measures and performance-based management techniques.
- Second, we will illustrate that a data-driven performance-based management process is not something that only large jurisdictions can implement. The methods that we tout can be implemented easily. It has been our experience that many jurisdictions already collect much of these data but do not organize them in a user-friendly

manner. We will show that election officials can implement their own performance-based management and evaluation systems – or work with others in their vicinity in a joint effort – with little difficulty.

Part of what is required to improve elections in the United States is a change in mind-set among all players in the elections policy arena. This includes not just state and local election officials but also members of Congress, state legislators, and county and city commissions who hold the purse strings of elections and make policy that often determines how elections are run. The election officials need to welcome the collection and dissemination of data and have some trust that the data they make public, and the openness that they engender, are used responsibly and appropriately. Academics and interest groups have to be willing to use data for more than mere "Gotcha! See how bad things are!" reports and instead use these data for analyses that help to promote effective public policy solutions to real election administration problems.

Finally, policy makers – the county commissioners and state legislators who are ultimately responsible for funding elections and making the laws that election administrators must implement – have to accept responsibility for the way in which elections are run and be willing to make policy decisions based on the best possible evidence, not based on gut reactions or partisanship. Often, these policy makers make laws without considering how they will be implemented and if there are appropriate resources available for the implementation to be successful. Performance data can improve decision making and help policy makers improve the performance of the electoral process.

In this book, we suggest a series of rigorous methods that can be used to produce responsible and appropriate evaluations of election performance and serve as practical performance measurement tools for improving election administration. These methods draw on previously implemented efforts to evaluate elections both in the United States and internationally as well as existing performance measurement tools that are used throughout the public and private sectors. It is important that these methods be designed using rigorous standards that ensure that the results of these studies are professional and meet the highest standards of research quality. The development of rigorous standards – and the potential for professional organizations to develop metrics and standards for performance evaluations and performance-based management research – will help discriminate legitimate research that represents a data-driven approach to electoral reform from advocacy work that represents a particular opinion.

This Is Not a Democracy Index

Recently, individuals frustrated with the slow pace of election reform have suggested utilizing data from election jurisdictions across the United States and reducing those data into some sort of simple Democracy Index. In the words of Heather Gerken (2009, 5), author of *The Democracy Index*, "the Index would function as the rough equivalent of the *U.S. News and World Report* rankings for colleges and graduate schools."

We are sympathetic to the goals of those who seek a Democracy Index, as they are asking that election officials provide to the public much of the sort of information and data that we also seek. We are also sympathetic to the overall goal of better understanding how different election jurisdictions perform, in the hope that we can apply practices that lead to superior election performance in states and counties that need improvement.

However, just as those who study higher education are critical of *U.S. News and World Report*'s annual rankings of colleges and universities, we are concerned that efforts to reduce election performance to a simplistic and combined grading scheme may not be very useful for improving the actual *management* of elections. As is the case with the annual rankings of colleges and universities, any effort to produce a Democracy Index will be heavily influenced by both the data that are available and how the data are manipulated to form an index. Take a simple example: let us say that we observe three different aspects of elections for every county in the United States in a presidential election: (1) voter turnout in the last election, (2) the percentage of provisional ballots cast of all ballots in the last election, and (3) the percentage of ballots that recorded no vote being cast in the presidential race.

On the basis of these three indicators, an index could be produced. Because an index produces a ranking, we might assume that higher rates of turnout are better, that lower rates of provisional ballot use are better, and that lower rates of unrecorded presidential ballots are better. Then counties that rank in the upper 20 percent on these three measures would get an A, those in the bottom 20 percent would get an F, and those in the middle would get a B, C, or D. But the highest-scoring jurisdiction may not provide the best election processes, in part because we do not have a standard to assess what those rates should be to determine a well-run election and in part because an index manipulates data based on a weighting scheme that is based on assumptions of quality that may be erroneous. Thus these grades could be useful, but there are also many problems with this approach, as we can illustrate using a couple of relatively simple examples.

First, it's really not clear whether "more is better" or "more is worse" with many indicators of election performance. Take the example of provisional ballots: is it always better that counties have lower rates of provisional ballot use? That's hard to say, because it is hard to know why voters are using provisional balloting. Consider two counties that both have high rates of provisional voting and two counties with low rates of provisional voting. County A might have high rates of provisional voting because it has a highly inaccurate voter registration system, so more provisional ballots reflect a systemic problem. Conversely, County B could have a high provisional vote rate because it has in place permissive rules regarding provisional balloting that substantially increase the number of these ballots. These two counties might have the same high provisional ballot rates but for very different reasons. On the other hand, County C might have an inaccurate voter registration system but also have restrictive procedures in place, making it difficult for voters to obtain a provisional ballot. In fact, the county's provisional vote rate might look the same as a jurisdiction with a very good registration system that is also slightly restrictive on how it has poll workers issue provisional ballots.

Now let us consider the example of turnout. Turnout may vary substantially based on the mobilization efforts of candidates, the competitiveness of various contests, and the amount of easily accessible information about the candidates (Downs 1957; Rosenstone and Hansen 1993). For example, presidential contests nearly always have higher turnout than off-year state and congressional elections, and turnout in a highly competitive electoral environment, like Ohio, will be higher than in a more one-party-dominant state like Utah. Does low turnout therefore indicate problems in election administration? It depends on the characteristics of the election players. Local election officials would likely prefer higher turnout to lower turnout, given the amount of energy and resources they put into elections, but, in general, are in a weak position to affect turnout. Moreover, a cross-sectional study of turnout would favor states or jurisdictions where competitive elections are more common or where registration barriers are low (e.g., EDR). The only way to know if turnout is a problem is to compare data over time from the same jurisdiction so that election context is held constant and anomalies can be easily identified.

As these examples show, it is not clear that one can readily reduce these outcomes to a simple grading scheme. It is only by examining electoral contexts continually over time, through an analysis of the training of the poll workers and the administrative rules or policies of the county clerk or local election official, that we can understand and interpret community and state data.

Second, it is difficult to know how to weight these three measures in an index. Should they be weighted equally, or should some indicators, like turnout, be weighted more than the others? Should these factors be weighted the same across states? It is hard to know because, ultimately, we are trying to use these three indicators to produce a measure of an abstract concept, election performance, which is not clearly defined and therefore difficult to quantify. Weighting is a key source of complaints when *U.S. News and World Report* issues its annual rankings of colleges and universities, and the same problem will arise in the production of a Democracy Index.

Third, being ranked on an index can produce perverse incentives. Once it is known what sort of indicators will be used in a Democracy Index, strategic election officials can manipulate their "score" by altering procedures – sometimes in potentially pernicious ways. For example, if the index uses a low rate of provisional ballots issued as a metric, then election officials who have high-quality registration systems but who have a permissive policy for issuing provisional ballots may develop increasingly restrictive policies about provisional ballot use. This could actually mean that fewer qualified voters get to cast ballots in such a jurisdiction.

The key issue with any index is whether governments have a means of productively addressing a low score on the index. In this regard, a Democracy Index can be unhelpful to the local election administrator located within a state with an inefficient legal framework. This jurisdiction, regardless of how well run it is, may be unable to improve its overall performance because of onerous laws. In this context, an index that scores the legal and structural barriers that exist at the *state* level that hinder effective election administration may be most valuable in, for example, states that have exceedingly restrictive laws that hinder voting by military personnel and overseas civilians, like the state of Alabama, or that have laws that systematically hamper the conduct of postelection audits, like Georgia's very short timeframe for certifying elections. Here the solution to having a low score is to improve the law so that it has greater facility. In the typical discussion of a Democracy Index, the idea of scoring laws is often overlooked or taken as being constant. However, for the election administrator, legal constraints may be a critical barrier to effective reform.

From Indexes to Performance-Based Management

Where a performance-based management process is more effective than a Democracy Index is in providing local election administrators with the tools they need to engage in continuous improvement of their elections. Any index will provide high-level measures of performance but will not generally provide administrators with the integrated data they need to improve management. As we discuss in this book, what administrators need are data that provide a multifaceted view on a problem. To go back to the provisional voting example, an effective performance-based management system will be able not only to tell election officials just how many provisional ballots are issued or rejected but also to provide information about the poll worker experience with provisional ballot training and implementation. Here it is the linkage between the cause and the outcome that is emphasized as opposed to just the outcome. For example, information on how many provisional ballots were rejected because of voter registration issues and how many were rejected because the voter or poll worker made an error in completing the provisional ballot form suggests different election administration problems and solutions.

By collecting data from poll workers and voters – as well as the various data produced throughout the election process – and analyzing these data systematically, election officials will be in a position to engage in what is commonly referred to as continuous performance improvement. Instead of focusing on the identification of problems after they occur, the goal of performance-based management and continuous improvement processes is to monitor the system and identify potential problems before they occur. If poll workers state that their training is weak, an election official would be able to resolve the training issues prior to having problems crop up in an election.

Our Book in Brief

In Chapter 1, we turn to a broad-brush discussion of our ecosystem approach for studying election performance, which is based on a number of similar applications in recent election cycles. Then, in Chapters 2–6, we examine the important components of a comprehensive ecological study of election performance, discussing data collection tools that can be used to examine the performance of a county, state, or even nation: data that are readily available to election officials (Chapter 2), information that comes from voter experience surveys (Chapter 3), poll worker surveys (Chapter 4), election administration process audits (Chapter 5), and qualitative observation-based monitoring studies (Chapter 6).

We then conclude our book by turning to a discussion of how election officials themselves can implement these performance studies or how they might work with others to conduct them. Finally, we discuss how our ecological approach to studying election performance provides information that should be used to frame both the assessment of recent elections and also provide feedback for improving the performance of future elections.

I

The Electoral Ecosystem

For most citizens, the exact operations of democratic government are a bit of a mystery. Ask even relatively well-informed citizens about how the U.S. Congress does its business, what precisely it is that a state lieutenant governor does on a daily basis, or when their local city council or school board meets, and you will likely get a shrug of the shoulders and "I'm not sure" in response. Countless surveys and studies have found that citizens can be very uninformed about how their government works (Delli Carpini and Keeter 1997).

This seems particularly true when it comes to one of the most important aspects of representative democracy: the administration of elections. Few voters are aware of what happens in the election prior to their receipt of a blank ballot – either a piece of paper or a direct recording electronic (DRE) voting machine screen – on which they are asked to vote. Few understand the logistics of sending out paper ballots as part of running an absentee balloting process, which is one of the fastest-growing methods of voting in the United States. They do not appreciate the complexity of the logistics of running early voting (another very quickly growing election process) or running Election Day precincts. Few voters – and not so many advocates and politicians! – have much of a clue about what happens to their ballot after they complete it and drop it in the ballot box, press "cast ballot" on the DRE, or drop their postal vote in a mailbox. A relatively small group of academics, advocates, candidates for public office (and the advisors who help them in that effort), and those who actually administer elections for their living appreciate the complexity of the process.

It might be hard to believe that so few people understand the processes involved in managing an election, but the situation today is much better than it was about a decade ago. Before the 2000 presidential election, especially prior to the near-meltdown of the election process in Florida, awareness about the general conduct of elections in the United States, and in other democratic nations around the world, was quite low. When the Florida situation became apparent on election night, academics like us were just as perplexed as everyone else by the seeming inability of election officials in the state to produce a clear and consistent tabulation of the presidential election vote. The most common book of reference that many people found on election administration during and after the Florida recount was Joseph Harris's *Election Administration in the United States*. The only problem was that Harris's book was written in 1934! In the days, weeks, months, and years since the 2000 election, political scientists, computer scientists, statisticians, law professors, and public policy experts have forged a new interdisciplinary research field that studies election technology and election administration.

As we have studied election technologies and administration, sometimes focusing on issues in a specific municipality's or county's election administration and in other cases focusing on the state or national level, we have found that there is not a well-developed approach for determining whether a given election was run well (also see Bjornlund 2004; Hyde 2010; Elklit and Reynolds 2005).[1] The problem is that there is no standard, no rule of thumb, to determine when problems, which almost always happen to one degree or another, reach a level that makes the entire election problematic. There are many discrete ways in which academics or observers have tried to quantitatively or qualitatively assess whether an election was run well. Typically, these measures will concern one feature of an election.

---

[1] The Carter Center, IFES, and the Office for Democratic Institutions and Human Rights at the Organization for Security and Co-operation in Europe do extensive election evaluations, but they are not the same type of management-focused evaluations that we are describing.

Election Observation

In recent decades, organizations such as the Carter Center, the International Federation for Electoral Systems (IFES), and the Organization for Security and Cooperation in Europe have pioneered the development of in-person election observation missions (Bjornlund 2004; Hyde 2010). These studies involve sending teams of trained personnel into a country to study an election, especially looking at the legal framework that governs the election as well as procedural issues and their implementation on Election Day. The in-person election observation methodology is one extremely valuable tool for the evaluation of elections. However, as the sole approach for studying the administration of an election, it is inadequate for many reasons: observers may not be able to study all aspects of an election, they cannot be in every voting location, they may not notice particular problems, they may be biased representatives, or they might be prevented from undertaking their assigned tasks; furthermore, in-person observation cannot say whether the official results at the end of election night are accurate (Hyde 2010; Brown 2005; Geisler 1993).

In addition, observers often have little training to prepare for the job and may not know the election administration rules in the local community; in addition, teams may lack consistency, decreasing the accuracy of their evaluations (Abbink and Van Binsbergen 2000; Carothers 1997; Pastor 1998). The observation process is also often unsystematic and nonrandom, contributing to problems in consistency and overall assessment of the process. Moreover, the election monitoring process in general does not include systematically gathered information from poll workers or voters regarding their experiences on Election Day.[2] As we discuss in later chapters, such data allow for problems in election administration to be triangulated and understood holistically.

Election Forensics

With the increase in interest regarding election results and the accuracy of election outcomes, there has arisen a new mode of election

---

[2] Some of these groups, such as IFES, have conducted such surveys on a limited basis.

evaluation: the postelection statistical analysis of electoral returns. These studies, now more commonly called *election forensics*, have proliferated in recent years, fueled by new statistical techniques, the greater availability of election data that can be analyzed, and fresh concerns about the integrity of elections. Researchers, armed with data on voter turnout or party votes, search for oddities in the data (see, e.g., Alvarez et al. 2008a; Mebane 2010; Wand et al. 2001). For example, voter mistakes in using the butterfly ballot in Palm Beach County, Florida, in 2000, created an overly high vote for presidential candidate Pat Buchanan (Brady et al. 2001b). Other examples of such oddities are elections with logically impossible results, such as turnout rates that exceed 100 percent, or patterns that do not compare well with realistic predictions, such as a solidly Republican district that suddenly elects (or almost elects) a Democrat (Levin et al. 2009; Myagkov et al. 2008).

Such forensics can be powerful tools, provided that the data used are accurate and available at the correct level of aggregation (e.g., precinct-level data, not state-level data) and that the researchers know which oddities to search for. For example, after the 2004 election, one study found that counties with high levels of Democratic Party registrations in northern Florida were voting Republican for president at high rates. The author did not seem to realize that there was a legacy of conservative Democrats in the South.[3] Election forensics tools, although powerful, cannot always be relied on solely to evaluate the overall performance of an election system. Rather than being a general performance diagnostic, they can only tell an observer if there are some indications of potential problems. Election forensics may not always reveal problems or the underlying causes of those problems. There are cases, such as in Palm Beach County, Florida, in 2001, where election forensics can identify the culprit. In that case, the butterfly ballot did it (Wand et al. 2001). A negative forensic result may not even be identifying problems at all; instead, it could merely be identifying statistical anomalies. Moreover, forensics is limited by the data used in the analyses, which are normally turnout and vote counts for each party. Such data limitations may

---

[3] See http://www.nytimes.com/2004/11/12/politics/12theory.html for a discussion of this study and its rebuttal.

also hamper the ability of researchers to identify the cause of many problems.

Legal Analysis

One critical aspect for understanding elections is to consider the legal framework within which the election occurs. The observer analyses noted earlier typically include a legal analysis, and Hall and Wang (2008) consider how such an analysis can be used to evaluate various aspects of an election. In evaluating an electoral system, the election law experts at the Mortiz College of Law have developed what they refer to as an *ecological systems model* for the evaluation of a state's election code. As they note in their report,

> a healthy election ecosystem should promote three core values: access, integrity, and finality. The value of access seeks to ensure that all citizens in our representative democracy can readily and equally participate in the selection of those who represent them (and in decisions regarding ballot issues). The value of integrity seeks to ensure that the election process occurs in a fair, accurate, and transparent manner that protects voter privacy and minimizes the potential for fraud. The value of finality recognizes that the outcomes of elections need to be determined expeditiously and conclusively. These values are sometimes in tension with one another, but a sound election ecosystem must serve them all.[4]

They go on to identify the nine key areas of elections to study: (1) institutional arrangements, (2) voter registration, (3) challenges to voter eligibility, (4) voting technology, (5) early and absentee voting, (6) polling place operations, (7) ballot security, (8) provisional voting, and (9) vote counting, recounting, and contests.

Such evaluations have not been conducted in the United States until recently but are an important part of understanding a state's electoral process. This type of study of a state's legal framework and the potential effects of a given legal framework on the implementation of elections on the ground can provide a strong baseline for evaluating an electoral system as they help us understand what the legally required processes, procedures, and requirements are for the election.

---

[4] See http://moritzlaw.osu.edu/electionlaw/projects/registration-to-recounts/book.pdf (page v), last accessed August 20, 2012.

Residual Votes

The most important initial analyses to come out of the 2000 election were the works related to residual voting.[5] A residual vote rate is computed by determining the total number of *ballots cast* in a given election race and subtracting the total number of *votes cast* in the race. The percentage of ballots that were cast without a vote for a given race is the residual vote rate for that race.[6] Residual vote studies are critical because they provide an easily understood metric for evaluating voting systems and voter understanding for how to use that system correctly. Although political science has long focused on turnout as the key metric for evaluating elections, turnout is irrelevant if the votes do not get counted; the residual vote metric evaluates the counting of votes. Several key works have identified variations in residual votes across voting technologies (e.g., Alvarez and Hall 2008b; Alvarez et al. 2008c; Ansolabehere and Stewart 2005; Caltech/MIT Voting Technology Project 2001a, 2001b); however, the more important works have examined residual votes in the context of communities with high numbers of minority and/or low-income voters (e.g., Stewart 2006; Herron and Sekhon 2005; Tomz and Van Houweling 2003). These studies have found that minority and low-income communities often have different experiences casting an accurate vote compared to more affluent or white communities.

There are, however, limitations to the residual vote rate – as currently used – as a metric for evaluating elections and voting technologies. Specifically, many jurisdictions across the country do not

---

[5] Residual votes are the uncounted ballots in an election, either overvotes or undervotes, or otherwise uncounted ballots. The key works in this area include Alvarez and Hall (2004, 2008b), Ansolabehere and Reeves (2012), Ansolabehere and Stewart (2005), Brady et al. (2001a), Buchler et al. (2004), Byrne et al. (2007), Caltech/MIT Voting Technology Project (2001a, 2001b), Card and Moretti (2007), Century Foundation (2004), Dee (2007), Everett et al. (2006), Frisina et al. (2008), Herrnson et al. (2008a, 2008b), Herron and Sekhon (2003, 2005), Herron and Wand (2007), Keating (2002), Knack and Kropf (2001, 2003a, 2003b), Internet Policy Institute (2001), Kimball and Kropf (2005, 2008), Mebane (2004), Norden et al. (2006), Sinclair and Alvarez (2004), Stein et al. (2008), Stewart (2004), Tomz and Van Houweling (2003), Hanmer et al. (2010), and Wand et al. (2001).

[6] E.g., if 100 ballots were cast in a mayoral race and there were 50 votes for Candidate A and 45 votes for Candidate B, then 5 ballots contained no vote that was counted for mayor. The residual vote rate would be 5%.

disaggregate data on ballots cast and votes cast by voting method. Absentee ballots, early-voting ballots, and precinct-cast ballots from Election Day are often combined in vote totals reported, even when some voters cast paper ballots by mail while others vote in person using electronic voting or electronic precinct tabulation of paper ballots. Combining results across different methods of voting may provide inaccurate information about residual vote rates in a jurisdiction attributable to a given voting technology or to the voter education efforts used to address residual vote issues.[7] Importantly, residual votes do not tell us about voter behavior. Although we know that there is top-of-the-ticket roll-off, we do not know how much of the variation is due to technology and how much is due to the preferences of the voter.

Postelection Audits

Concerns about security of voting systems (see, e.g., Kohno et al. 2004) have led to the creation of a second metric: the postelection ballot comparison, often referred to as a *postelection audit* or *vote tabulation audit*. The vote tabulation audit has existed since the advent of electronic tabulation of paper ballots. There are two key goals behind vote tabulation audits. The primary goal is to test the accuracy of the electronic ballot count by the computerized vote tabulators by taking a sample of the paper ballots that were electronically tabulated and hand counting them to determine if the ballots were counted correctly. The second goal is to identify the causes of discrepancies between the reported vote from the machine and voter intent. This latter goal is a bit more reflective and focuses on process improvement, including the design of more effective paper ballots and voter education. However, most state laws do not focus on reporting these problems and investigating them fully. Sometimes these audits yield interesting differences between the results of the paper count and the electronic count, which are often attributable to either problems humans have

---

[7] Education is a critical component of lowering residual votes, especially if the jurisdiction does not use any form of in-precinct electronic feedback to the voter about problems with their ballots. The Help America Vote Act explicitly requires extensive voter education efforts in these situations.

counting paper or problems voters have marking a ballot correctly so that it can be counted by the tabulator (see, e.g., Atkeson et al. 2008b). The information from these audits can often inform us about the relative effectiveness with which the first election count was conducted and can notify us as to whether the election counts were in some way anomalous.[8]

There is an argument as to whether these postelection audits are meaningful if there has not been appropriate consideration given to auditing the entire election.[9] Quite simply, one can ask whether the results of a postelection audit of ballots are meaningful if the chain of custody for the ballots has not been audited. If the chain of custody has been violated, it could be that the results of the audit are meaningless because the ballots audited are not authentic (Alvarez and Hall 2008b). Audits in a more general context, such as in business or government, typically involve more than the comparison of two tallies; instead, they involve the evaluation of processes, procedures, training, and systems that produce the tallies in question (as well as considering the two-tally comparison that is the hallmark of the vote tabulation audit). As Bouckaert and Peters (2002) have noted, measuring performance is often closely linked to auditing, given that effective audits require having in place a comprehensive system for collecting data and measuring organizational performance in achieving key tasks.

Voter Surveys

More recently, scholars have begun to study the attitudes and behaviors of voters with regard to their election experiences.[10] Understanding the voter experience is a critical component of election evaluation

---

[8] Election auditing is the subject of a volume of essays we have edited and contributed. See Alvarez, Atkeson, and Hall (2012).

[9] See Alvarez, Atkeson, and Hall (2012) regarding the fact that election audits should be much more comprehensive to be meaningful.

[10] See, e.g., Alvarez et al. (2007a); "The 2006 New Mexico Election Administration Report," typescript, University of New Mexico, http://www.unm.edu/~atkeson/newmexico.html; Ansolabehere (2007, 2008a, 2008b); Magleby et al. (2007); Atkeson et al. (2010c); "Assessing Electoral Performance in New Mexico in 2008 Using an Ecosystem Approach," typescript, University of New Mexico, http://www.unm.edu/~atkeson/newmexico.html; Atkeson et al. (2011a); "The 2010 New Mexico Election Administration Report," typescript, University of New Mexico, http://www.unm.edu/~atkeson/newmexico.html.

because voters are the clients in the election administration process, and information about the voter experience can identify procedural issues, problems in training of poll workers, voter education issues, places where legislative action might be necessary, areas where better communication with voters is necessary, problems with the ballot, or problems with different voting modes (e.g., absentee vs. in person).

These studies can be important for identifying specific election administration failures. For example, asking a voter for identification when the state does not have a voter identification requirement is an indication of poll worker training problems (Atkeson et al. 2010a; Ansolabehere 2008a; Cobb et al. 2012). Likewise, voter reports of balloting problems, a lack of privacy, and long lines suggest that there may have been training or polling place management problems that interfered with the effective running of the voting process in a given jurisdiction.

Starting in 2001, political scientists began asking a very simple set of questions on national, statewide, and local surveys as well as exit polls about voter confidence, the counting of ballots, the types of voting technologies voters preferred, and the voting equipment they had used historically (Bullock et al. 2005; Alvarez et al. 2007b, 2008b, 2009b, 2010; Atkeson and Saunders 2007; Atkeson et al. 2010d). The interest in voter confidence stems from the very visible problems in the election process in the 2000 election and from other studies on how election administration might affect voter evaluations of the voting process (e.g., Wand et al. 2001; Tomz and Van Houweling 2003; Sinclair and Alvarez 2004; Hall et al. 2009; Atkeson et al. 2010c). These observed problems in the performance of recent elections in the United States have led scholars and policy makers alike to examine whether these problems have affected the perceptions of citizens and voters about the integrity and legitimacy of election outcomes.

These data have provided a baseline for understanding the factors that affect the confidence of voters, especially race, party affiliation, voting mode, and the importance of the interaction of voters with poll workers and the ballots. Voter confidence is important as African American voters tend to be less confident than whites (Alvarez et al. 2007b, 2008b, 2009b; Bullock et al. 2005), although this was not the case in 2008 (Alvarez et al. 2009b), and Hispanics do not appear to have any difference in voter confidence from whites (Atkeson and Saunders 2007; Atkeson et al. 2010c). Partisan losers of the election are typically less confident than partisan winners (Democrats were less confident than Republicans in 2000 and 2004 but more confident in 2008) (Bullock et al. 2005; Alvarez et al. 2008b). In addition, voters who cast ballots absentee are less confident than precinct voters (Atkeson and Saunders 2007; Alvarez et al. 2008b; Bryant 2010; Atkeson et al. 2011a). Other analyses show that the local election experience matters to voter confidence. Voters' interactions with poll workers lead to greater confidence, but a confusing ballot leads to lower voter confidence (Atkeson and Saunders 2007; Hall et al. 2009). More recent survey research using data from the Congressional Election Study (CES) has found that voter confidence also has preelection and postelection components. Before the election, confidence is shaped by the voter's experience in the most recent election as well as by socioeconomic factors. Postelection, voter confidence can change based on the results of the election and if the voter cast a ballot for the winning or losing party (Alvarez et al. 2009b).

In 2007, 2008, and 2009, the Caltech/MIT Voting Technology Project – in conjunction with the Pew Charitable Trusts's Make Voting Work Initiative – conducted the Survey of the Performance of American Elections (Alvarez et al. 2009a). In this study, 200 registered voters in each of the 50 states (10,000 respondents in total) were surveyed and asked about their experience in the 2008 general election. The survey asked if a person voted and then asked either (1) why he or she did not vote or (2) how the quality of his or her voting experience was (either in person or absentee by mail). The goal of the survey was to determine, at a state level, what people experienced when they voted in the election. For instance, the voters who voted in person were asked first if they voted in person on Election Day or early or if they voted absentee. In-person voters were asked if they encountered problems with their voter registration, the voting equipment, or finding their polling place. They were also asked about their confidence that their vote was counted accurately and to rate the quality of their poll workers. These studies provide, at the state level, an understanding of the issues associated with voting in the 2008 election.

Poll Worker Surveys

Surveying voters has the benefit of identifying the quality of the voting experience as perceived by the voter. Similar benefits accrue from surveying poll workers about their experiences with the election (Hall et al. 2007, 2008; Alvarez et al. 2007a, 2010; Atkeson et al. 2010c, 2011a). For example, by surveying poll workers, it is possible to determine how descriptively similar the poll workers are in relationship to the population they serve, the quality of the training they received, the difficulties they encountered on Election Day, and any systematic problems – such as with ballot security – that can affect the outcome of the election. As with voter surveys, it is possible to use poll worker surveys to identify the correlates that exist between the election work experience and confidence in the electoral process. Training is one key correlate, as is the technological sophistication of the poll worker. It is also possible to determine why poll workers do some of the things they do that may be contrary to the law or procedural requirements. To continue with the example of asking for identification at the polls, poll workers may ask for identification because it is loud in the polling place, because they have difficulty hearing, or because they mistakenly think they are required to get identification from some people or everyone. Although each item may be incongruous to the law, each possible option also gives election officials and observers important information about why there has been a procedural breakdown.

Incident Reports

Related to the surveying of poll workers is the capturing of poll worker experience data through Election Day incident reports. Such reports can be captured at the precinct level (e.g., Kiewiet et al. 2008; Odegard 2009) or at the local election office level through logs of calls received from poll workers to the central office on Election Day. As Kiewiet et al. (2008) discovered, incident report data can identify the level of systematic problems, the randomness of problems, and the possibility that fraud may have occurred. However, one problem with incident reports is the lack of consistency in their use between precinct poll workers. Some poll workers provide detailed notes on everything that happened over the course of the day, whereas others provide very little information. Thus, as a systematic tool, incident reports have some weaknesses, but anecdotally, they can provide useful and corroborating information.

Improving Performance: One Measure Does Not Work

Many approaches have been used in the past decade to study the performance of an election system: residual votes, survey measures of voter and poll worker confidence, the results of postelection audits, and evaluations of the legal apparatus that supports election administration. By themselves, they are helpful diagnostics, but more can be done to use these data for improving the performance and management of elections, as we discuss throughout this book.

The various metrics for evaluating elections and the issues associated with their implementation were outlined earlier. Each of these different evaluation metrics is important individually, but together, they allow for election issues to be evaluated using triangulation. Triangulation is the idea that by combining multiple measures to evaluate an election, a more holistic evaluation of the administrative process can be conducted and the correlates of trust, confidence, and quality can be identified. As all the methods we described have inherent weaknesses and biases, the ability to confidently affirm or disaffirm strengths and weaknesses of an election is enhanced with the use of multiple methods (Webb et al. 1966; Singleton et al. 1988). The value of triangulation, as Singleton et al. (1988, 361) state,

is the use of dissimilar methods or measures, which do not share the same methodological weaknesses – that is, errors and biases. The observations ... produced by each method will ordinarily contain some error. But if the pattern of error varies, as it should with different methods, and if these methods independently produce or "zero-in" on the same findings, then our confidence in the result increases.

Triangulation, therefore, is an important way to cross-validate research.

Figure 1.1 illustrates the various metrics for election evaluation discussed previously. Where two or more metrics are used at the same time, an overlap is created that allows for multiple considerations of

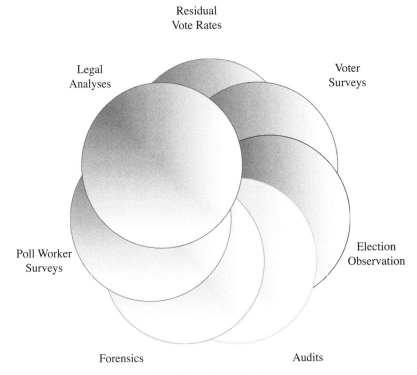

Residual
Vote Rates

Legal
Analyses

Voter
Surveys

Poll Worker
Surveys

Election
Observation

Forensics

Audits

FIGURE 1.1. Performance-based election evaluations.

the same concept. For example, if voters say in a voter survey that there were long lines at the polls, this fact is now known, but the reason why the lines occurred is not. One might attempt to correlate lines with voting technology used to determine if that is the cause of the lines. Such a finding would be logical because electronic voting has been shown in some studies to "push" voters through a ballot more fully than is the case with paper ballots, where voters can skip races easily. However, election observation may find that the lines in the election were the result of some problem with voter registration or with not having enough ballots, not with voting machines. A poll worker survey may reinforce that poll workers reported difficulties with the voter registration system. For example, demographic and work data from the poll worker survey may show that the poll workers who worked the voter registration process in a state with electronic voting were the oldest and least technologically savvy because the election officials in the state were worried about having these older, technophobic workers interacting with the voting machines.

As each performance metric is layered onto other performance metrics, a more holistic picture of the overall management and processes from the election emerges. Because these metrics typically use different data sources – from surveys, audits, election results, historical data, and third-party observation – each new data metric can assist in the validation of another metric. Problems or successes identified by one metric can be clarified and better understood based on the data from another metric. This multidimensionality is important in the current election environment, where claims and counterclaims are frequently made about the efficacy (or lack thereof) of various aspects of election administration or various voting technologies. Each performance metric informs the process more, cr eating a cycle of information that can lead to better policy changes. Election officials and others can know if key performance goals are being met and where successes and failures are occurring. Evaluations of voters, polling places, and poll workers, for example, might identify issues that are addressed in changes to the law and in changes to training or procedures. These new changes, in turn, can be evaluated for their efficacy.

The second key reason for using a holistic approach is that it enables election officials to better understand their election environments and allows policy makers to effectively gauge the health of their election administration systems when, as part of a highly effective local or state government performance-based management system, these metrics, in combination, allow election officials to evaluate their administrative processes and standard operating procedures they use for running elections. Where problems are identified, a holistic approach may suggest places where training should be improved, voter information or education should be enhanced, new procedures should be put in place, or new voting systems should be considered. This is also of importance to election officials as they interact with interest groups and the claims that such groups make about election administration. For example, Los Angeles County, California, created a Community Voter Outreach Committee to facilitate interactions with various interest groups, including language minorities in the county, who often complained about the way in which the county administered elections.

An effective mechanism for using election administration information gathered by interest groups allowed the county to work with groups to address their concerns systematically (Hall 2003). Having sound data is the best way to address the claims that these groups make, either by refuting claims or by allowing these claims to be validated and addressed.

The New Mexico Example

One example of a holistic study that uses multiple methods for studying the performance of the electoral system is the 2006 election administration study in New Mexico.[11] This study combined information about election reform from the perspectives of voters, election workers, and professional observers on the ground on Election Day in three New Mexico counties.[12] This study produced a report about election administration in New Mexico and has been used in New Mexico as the basis for significant policy changes to election administration practices at the state and local levels and to changes in New Mexico election law. The data generated by this study allowed the authors to isolate both the successes and failures of the New Mexico election experience in 2006.

The study examined the implementation of a new paper-based voting system to determine how well the election system worked around this new technology. From the election observation data and surveys, it was determined that there was a need to improve ballot security and voter privacy, to promote uniformity in election administration procedures across precincts, to develop postprocedure election audits and ballot reconciliation procedures, to improve ballot design, and to better educate voters.

Voters in Bernalillo County, the largest county in the state, representing about one-third of voters, indicated that their confidence in their votes being counted was quite high: more than 80 percent were very or somewhat confident. Among poll workers, more than 90 percent were very or somewhat confident. Both poll workers and voters

---

[11] See Alvarez et al. (2007a).
[12] The voter survey in 2006 was only done in the First Congressional District. Later studies in 2008 and 2010 implemented statewide voter surveys.

rated the overall performance of their poll workers high: 86.9 percent of voters rated their poll workers as very or somewhat helpful, and almost 75 percent of poll workers rated their fellow poll workers highly. Voters and poll worker data also indicate that both groups were largely favorable to the new voting process.

One of the key findings of this study was that although most polling places were free of systematic problems on Election Day, certain precincts were fraught with problems. Specifically, the survey of poll workers found that most polling locations had the supplies and workers they needed, but a small minority of poll workers reported that they did not have the supplies (13.8%) or workers (17.4%) needed to do the job. Most polling places were in good or excellent condition to perform their duties, but a small minority, roughly 1 in 10, were in poor or very poor condition.

One of the important points of triangulation was on the question of voter identification. The voter survey found that Hispanic and male voters were more likely to show some form of voter identification at the polls than were non-Hispanics and women (Atkeson et al 2010c). This finding is problematic on its face; it suggests bias in the implementation of the state voter identification law. The data from the poll worker survey confirmed that many poll workers did not understand the voter identification laws, and many poll workers asked voters for identification for reasons other than required by law. Election monitors also observed the incorrect implementation of the voter identification laws.

The triangulation of data also showed that one initial explanation for the bias toward asking Hispanic voters for identification more than white voters, a racial bias by white poll workers, was false. The data from this study found that both white and Hispanic poll workers were equally likely to ask male and Hispanic voters to show identification. With the additional information, it was possible to see that the answer to the problem was more complex than one of mere bias.

One benefit of the findings was that they resulted in changes in state policy in New Mexico and local election administration. During the legislative session of 2007, the law was changed to simplify voter identification rules, removing the requirement that voters need to know the last four numbers of their Social Security number. Second, the secretary of state ordered that rules regarding voter identification be posted in each polling location and developed a poster explaining the rules that was to be hung in each polling station. At the local level, county clerks worked to improve their training on this issue and instituted other changes in their election administration as a result of other findings in the report.

Cuyahoga County Example

In 2006, the Election Science Institute conducted a comprehensive study of election administration in Cuyahoga County, Ohio. Much like the study in New Mexico, the study followed the transition to a new voting system (from punch cards to touch screen voting) and also combined a poll worker survey, a voter exit poll, and election observations conducted through an incident reporting process. The voter study examined attitudes about the voting experience and the voting technology. In addition to asking about attitudes toward the voting technology, the survey asked about the voter experience in the polling place, including wait times for voting, experiences with poll workers, and other attributes of the polling place.

The exit poll found that roughly 90 percent of voters liked the new system, and similar percentages were confident that their votes would be counted accurately. Although there were high levels of confidence, one very important finding was that voters who election officials might worry would have trouble with the transition, such as older voters, thought the system was easier to use. Specifically, 95 percent of elderly voters and almost 90 percent of African American voters reported that touch screen voting was easier than voting using punch cards.

These findings are interesting in isolation. However, they become especially interesting when compared to the experience of poll workers on Election Day. For a sizable minority of poll workers, the transition to electronic voting was anything but simple. Almost one-third of poll workers reported that there were difficulties opening the polls because of issues with the voting machines. During the day, 38 percent of poll workers reported some difficulty with the VVPAT printers. At the end of Election Day, 45 percent of poll workers reported having difficulties closing down the machines. Not surprisingly, given these findings, poll workers found that the training that they received prior to the election was less than adequate. Specifically, in the poll worker survey, just over 40 percent of poll workers reported differences between the training that they received regarding how to use the voting machines and the actual operation of the machines on Election Day. The differences

reported were large; 74 percent of the poll workers who reported differences between training and their experience said that the differences
were relatively large (a lot different or somewhat different). The training was given very low scores on a variety of levels, with more than
half of poll workers saying that the training did not give them enough
information to do their job well, nor did it provide enough hands-on
experience. Given this problem with training, it is even more problematic that half of all poll workers had to call the county's Election Day
command center on Election Day.

The results of the poll worker survey were made clearer still by
the incident report data. The incident reports showed that 89 percent
of all precincts reported at least one incident, with almost 10 percent
of precincts reporting 10 or more incidents. The incidents were not
all machine related; in fact, the most common problems were incidents involving voter registration issues (30%). Machine problems
were the second most common problem (16%); 9 percent of all incidents reported related to the poll workers themselves – typically, a
worker not showing up for work. Interestingly, there was a positive
correlation between poll worker incidents (not showing up) and more
claims of other problems. This suggests that when a precinct is missing
poll workers, it is susceptible to other problems occurring.

Again, we see in the Cuyahoga case that the problems that would
be identified with any given mode of study would give a different
answer to the question, how was the election? From the voter's perspective, the answer was, "I was confident that the votes were counted
correctly." From the poll worker surveys, there were clearly problems with the training and the voting machine information. From the
incident reports, voter registration was clearly a problem. The triangulation tells us that the problems were across the board and provides
a more gloabl understanding of the Election Day voting experience.

Improving the Ecosystem

This chapter illustrates the numerous methods that can be used to
evaluate the performance of elections in the United States. However,
many of the studies noted here are one–off efforts or studies that were
conducted for academic purposes. Even the studies in New Mexico and
Cuyahoga County, which were very robust studies, were not part of

an integrated election management process. For elections to improve systematically, the data and methods we have discussed have to be part of an overall process of evaluation, feedback, and improvement. Data on various performance measures have to be used consistently for policy and management purposes.

The benefits of performance-based management can be considered by asking the following questions about Cuyahoga County, based on the study noted previously:

1. Was the 2006 general election in Cuyahoga County better managed compared to the 2006 primary election?
2. Were the changes to policies, training, and procedures implemented after the 2006 primary election effective in improving the election processes for poll workers?
3. Was the 2008 primary election better implemented compared to the 2006 primary election, as measured by problems at the polls, voter confidence, poll worker confidence, and residual vote rates?
4. Did voter and poll worker confidence change after the 2006 general election or after the media coverage of the problems in the 2006 primary election?
5. What is the status of the performance of the Cuyahoga County election office today?

The answer to all these questions is – using the metrics we have described in this book – we do not know. We cannot know if voters are more or less confident, if they have had better or worse experiences, if poll worker training is better or worse, if poll workers are more or less confident, if residual vote rates across various modes of voting are increasing or decreasing (although this can be easily calculated), or if other issues with voting and technology have improved or deteriorated.

Not having these data puts the election managers in Cuyahoga County – the election manager and the deputy manager – and senior policy makers (the Cuyahoga County Board of Election and the secretary of state) at a severe disadvantage in knowing if their efforts and policy changes are actually improving things. They can have some idea, based on anecdotal evidence, from reviewing the documents used in the election canvass and other sources, but unless they collect and analyze data systematically and repeatedly, it is very difficult to know if things are improving. Moreover, it is difficult to know *why* they are improving. For example, new poll worker training may coincide with a decline in a certain problem at the polls, but poll workers may find the new training confusing, and the problem may be decreasing for another reason. Likewise, when the Boards of Election want to appeal for a legal change from the Ohio legislature, having systematic data would definitely improve their ability to make a sustained, detailed argument for why certain changes should be implemented.

Conclusions

The use of performance data can vastly improve the ability of election officials to manage the election process and target resources effectively. An array of data can be collected and an array of methods can be used to analyze these data. Many of these data are simple to collect, simple to analyze, and easy to act on when problems are identified. The studies in New Mexico and Cuyahoga County both show that such projects can be done and that important findings can arise from these studies.

The problem that exists today is that these data are rarely collected in a regularized, sustained manner. Unless jurisdictions do this, they are left in a situation where they have a twofold deficit. First, they have data on hand that are being underutilized. Some data exist, but they are not being used systematically, as performance metrics, to address management and process improvement questions. Second, they are working in a policy environment where they are unable to repeatedly evaluate the true performance of their organization. They have only a limited, cross-sectional view of past performance, potential threats, and what the future may portend.

Effective organizations can only be effective if they know (1) what they do, (2) how they do what they do, and (3) how well they do what they do. Without data and metrics, election officials are at a disadvantage because, in the political and media-intense environment in which they operate, interest groups and other players bring their own data and analyses to the debate over performance. Unless election officials have effective methods of capturing data in a regularized way, they cannot respond to concerns brought to the debate or explain how their proposed reforms will improve elections in the future.

2

Easily Available Data for Performance Evaluation

The first question that arose in the immediate aftermath of the 2000 presidential election, when we started to study the performance of election processes in the United States, was a simple one: what data were readily available that could be used to assess the problems seen in the election, especially in Florida? That question led those of us who were involved in the early stages of the Caltech/MIT Voting Technology Project (VTP) to focus on the measure called the *residual vote* – a measure that we now see as a vital and readily available gauge of the accuracy and reliability of voting technologies.

However, as we discussed in the first two chapters of this book, there are other readily available sources of election performance data that election officials routinely collect but typically do not employ in a broader and more comprehensive performance-based management and evaluation process. These data form the basis for developing a set of indicators that can be used to assess the performance of elections in a given jurisdiction and the backbone for a performance-based management system that can be used to engage in ongoing quality improvements of the electoral process.

In this chapter, we will discuss a number of those, including provisional voting data, incident reports and security evaluations, and the foundation of the election administration system: the voter registration file. We then discuss how these systems can be used to create a performance-based management system for monitoring the performance of elections at the state and local levels in the United States.

By no means is this a comprehensive discussion; other sources of information are often routinely collected by election officials but not then deployed for subsequent performance evaluations such as the results of audits and recounts. No doubt there are others, and as we argue in the conclusion to this chapter, election officials should keep their eyes open for all ways in which routine operations generate information or data that can be used to gauge the effectiveness of their processes.

The Residual Vote

When the VTP researchers set out to conduct their first analysis of voting technologies, a particular focus was examining their reliability and accuracy, as those were the primary concerns coming out of the 2000 presidential election in Florida. They had to use the data they were able to gather to develop measurement approaches that would let them determine which voting technologies were more reliable and accurate and which were less reliable and accurate.

The primary responsibility for administering elections in the United States falls on state governments (Karlan and Ortiz 2002). In practice, in most states, counties and sometimes municipalities have the primary responsibility for conducting elections. The multiplicity of election administration authorities makes collecting any type of election performance data complicated. In addition, the regulations and procedures for the systematic collection and reporting of data about any particular election are inconsistent across states and are sometimes inconsistent across local election jurisdictions within a particular state (Alvarez et al. 2005). These factors made it very difficult to collect a critical piece of data needed to evaluate voting technology: what type of voting system was used in a particular jurisdiction? As luck would have it, a private election data company (Election Data Services Inc.) had been collecting this information in the United States before the 2000 presidential election, and we were able to reach an arrangement to get access to the data it had collected.[1]

---

[1] The relative difficulty the VTP faced collecting these important data in 2000 led us to a recommendation for the creation of a federal entity that would collect and disseminate data like this. The 2002 HAVA created such an entity – the U.S. Election Assistance Commission (EAC). Since 2004, the EAC has worked to collect and distribute data about election administration (see http://www.eac.gov/program-areas/research-resources-and-reports/completed-research-and-reports/election-day-survey-results).

TABLE 2.1. *Residual Votes as a Percentage of All Ballots Cast, 1988–2000*

Machine Type	President	Governor or Senator
Paper ballot	1.8	3.3
Punch card	2.5	4.7
Optical scan	1.5	3.5
Lever machine	1.5	7.6
Electronic (DRE)	2.3	5.9

Knowing each election jurisdiction's voting technology (typically at the county level), we then needed to devise a measure of the voting system's performance as observed at that same geographic level. Although the data reporting was far from perfect, many state and local election jurisdictions in 2000 either reported or were willing to provide to VTP researchers the number of ballots cast in the 2000 election and the number of ballots counted in races on the ballot. Shockingly, several states were not able to provide these data because they did not – and some still do not – collect data on the number of ballots cast in an election. Armed with these data, VTP researchers were able to develop a performance measure termed the residual vote. A residual vote is computed simply as the percentage of ballots cast that did not record a vote in a particular race (the number of votes in a given race divided by the total number of votes cast). In our initial analyses, the VTP studied the two statewide races at the top of the ballot in each location: the presidential race and then either the gubernatorial or U.S. Senate race (Caltech/MIT Voting Technology Project 2001a, 2001b).

Table 2.1 reproduces the estimates of the residual vote, by voting technology, reported by the VTP in 2001 (Caltech/MIT Voting Technology Project 2001b, 21). This simple analysis led to a number of important conclusions. Generally, we found that optical scan paper ballots had the lowest rate of residual votes, while punch card systems had the highest residual vote in presidential elections of any voting technology. We estimated that more than 30 million voters used punch card voting systems in the 2000 presidential election, and these results imply that had these voters used an optical scan voting system, 300,000 more votes would have been counted in the presidential race, and 420,000 more votes would have been counted in the Senate and gubernatorial races. The high residual vote rate that we found for punch card and lever voting machines led us to recommend that they be phased out, a recommendation that was incorporated into the 2002 Help America Vote Act (HAVA).

Subsequently, the concept of a residual vote has been widely used in many studies. For example, researchers have used the residual vote to study how factors other than voting technology are related to residual vote rates (e.g., Ansolabehere 2002; Sinclair and Alvarez 2004). Stewart (2006) used the residual vote measure to assess the effects of voting technology innovations. Between 2000 and 2004, many counties replaced their old voting systems and adopted a new voting system, and Stewart took advantage of those innovations to assess the reduction in residual votes when election jurisdictions acquired new voting systems. Using the year 2000 as a baseline, Stewart found that the largest change in the residual vote rate came in jurisdictions that transitioned from punch cards to electronic voting systems. This switch resulted in a 1.61 percentage point reduction in residual votes. The second greatest reduction in residual votes came in jurisdictions that transitioned from optical scan to electronic voting systems (a 1.23 percentage point reduction). The third greatest reduction was in jurisdictions that transitioned from punch cards to optical scanning (a 1.09 percentage point reduction). Changing voting systems reduced residual vote rates.

Of course, the residual vote measure is far from perfect, as has been pointed out by researchers who employ it (Alvarez et al. 2005). It represents all undervotes and overvotes and, therefore, cannot distinguish between intentional nonvoting by a voter in a given race from a voter who made an error on the ballot or from a voting machine malfunction. In addition, it could not determine if voters were voting incorrectly as was the case with the butterfly ballot in 2000 in Palm Beach County, Florida. Despite these flaws, it does represent a measure that can be computed easily using comparable data, and these data are increasingly available from election officials.

Residual vote data also provide a clear performance metric that can be used for improving elections. A jurisdiction can use residual vote data to identify if there are voting problems across precincts in a jurisdiction and differences in voting experiences between in-person and absentee voting. For example, Alvarez et al. (2011) have found that residual vote rates are higher in California among absentee voters compared to in-person voters. This performance metric suggests that there may need to be better voter education regarding how to cast an accurate absentee ballot. Variations across precincts, within a jurisdiction, could also be a sign of a need for better voter or poll worker education or a failure of voting technologies in certain precincts.

Provisional Ballots: Multiple Metrics

Although provisional ballots are important for helping voters to have an opportunity to cast a ballot in a situation where their names are not in the voter roll, data on who votes using provisional balloting can also help election officials better understand the performance of a variety of aspects of their jurisdictions' voting systems. There are a variety of ways in which provisional balloting data, used with caution, can provide multiple metrics for evaluating the performance of an election administration system and the effectiveness of election processes.

According to a study by the Pew Charitable Trust, in the 2008 presidential election, there were over 2 million provisional ballots cast. Of those, about 70 percent were eventually included in final tabulations of results, and 30 percent were not counted.[2] At the state level, there was considerable variance in the data reported in the Pew study. For example, in Arizona, 6.61 percent of ballots cast in the 2008 presidential election were provisional, but in Wisconsin, the rate was 0.01 percent. Arizona had the highest and Wisconsin the lowest provisional ballot rate in the Pew analysis. The Pew analysis did not explore why there is so much variation across states, but it is likely a function of procedural and regulatory differences in state law and local implementation of these laws.[3] For example, three of the states with the lowest rates of provisional ballot use allow for Election Day voter registration. These states have little use for provisional ballots because voter registration problems can be addressed through registration on Election Day. Provisional voters would fall into a narrow category of individuals

---

[2] The Pew Center on the States, "Provisional Ballots: An Imperfect Solution," July 2009, http://www.pewcenteronthestates.org/uploadedFiles/ELEC_ProvBallot_Brief_0709.pdf.

[3] Determining exactly which state-level factors led to higher or lower provisional ballot rates is a very important research question regarding the performance of the election systems across states but is one we will not pursue here.

who were unlikely to be qualified to vote for other reasons.[4] However, without additional analysis, it is difficult to be certain whether Election Day voter registration, or other procedures, explains the differences observed across the states in provisional ballot use in the 2008 presidential election.[5]

As part of this Pew research project, we contributed two studies: one analyzing provisional ballot use across counties in New Mexico and one analyzing county-level data from Ohio.[6] In the New Mexico study, our analysis of provisional balloting data from 2008 found a number of important results that speak volumes about county-by-county election performance in the state. For example, most of the provisional ballots that were counted came from Election Day voters (58.1%), and the bulk of the remainder were from "in-lieu of" voters.[7] We undertook additional analysis of the New Mexico provisional voting data, both across counties as well as within Santa Fe County, using detailed data that contained reasons why provisional ballots were rejected.

For our purposes here, it is important to note our conclusions based on this analysis:

The New Mexico experience with provisional ballots suggests that rules, poll worker training, and voter education matter. Simple instructions not being followed during processing can result in a ballot's disqualification. Well-trained poll workers are more likely to process provisional ballots appropriately, reducing the risk of ballot disqualification. Voters also need to understand the rules to ensure that they meet the necessary conditions of a qualified voter.

This demonstrates the great utility that provisional balloting data, when analyzed within a specific county, and across counties within a state, can provide to election officials and stakeholders who wish to better understand the performance of their election process. Note also how provisional voting data can provide numerous performance-based

[4] E.g., an otherwise qualified individual might not meet a state's residency requirement for eligibility.
[5] Wisconsin, Maine, and Wyoming have Election Day voter registration; their provisional balloting rates were 0.01%, 0.01%, and 0.02%, respectively.
[6] "Provisional Voting in New Mexico," http://www.pewcenteronthestates.org/report_detail.aspx?id=54834; "Provisional Ballots in the 2008 Ohio General Election," http://www.pewcenteronthestates.org/report_detail.aspx?id=54835.
[7] In-lieu of voters are individuals who were sent an absentee ballot but decided to vote on Election Day and did not bring their unmarked absentee ballot to the precinct to exchange for an Election Day ballot. Provisional balloting is used to ensure that such voters do not vote twice.

management metrics. The reasons for provisional voting provide information about voter education – do voters know where their polling place is? – and the efficacy of the voter registration list itself. Also, it provides an important metric for evaluating poll workers. Errors on the provisional ballot envelopes suggest problems with the training that poll workers received and their ability to complete the outer envelope form.

Incident Reports and Poll Worker Feedback

As we have worked with election officials and studied election administration in the past decade, we have found that quite frequently, election officials have in place some means for poll workers and precinct rovers, who address problems in a set of precincts on Election Day, to provide feedback about how the election went in their location. In some cases, these feedback forms are quite general – literally a sheet of paper with a line at the top asking that poll workers write down any problems they encountered in their voting location. In other cases, these forms are more detailed, asking specific questions that are of interest to election administrators. Some jurisdictions even conduct surveys or debriefings of precinct captains after the election to get feedback on the way the election was run.

These feedback forms or incident reports are another underutilized source of important information and data that can be used in comprehensive election performance analysis. Unfortunately, it is not generally the case that these reports are systematically studied after an election to determine what can be learned from them. The problem is that these reports have not been structured to provide metrics that can be integrated with other data from the election to provide more nuanced indications of issues that have arisen in an election.

How can incident reports provide performance metrics? An interesting opportunity to examine this question came as part of a study in Cuyahoga County, Ohio, in the May 2006 election (the same study noted in Chapter 2).[8] The precinct incident reports were obtained from

---

[8] The study was overseen by the Election Science Institute. Details of the study can be found in "DRE Analysis for May 2006 Primary, Cuyahoga County, Ohio," http://moritzlaw.osu.edu/electionlaw/news/documents/DREAnalysisforMay2006 Primary.pdf.

1,216 of the 1,435 Election Day precincts from the 2006 May primary election in Cuyahoga County. The one-page forms simply asked poll workers to provide their estimate of the average and longest voter wait times and to then document any problems they encountered during the election. These forms were transcribed into an electronic database, and the transcriptions were then coded into a quantitative database.[9]

These incident reports produced important data that exposed an array of issues that arose on Election Day. For example, most precincts reported 4 incidents or fewer, but a small number reported 10 incidents or more. Additionally, when the type of incident reported was analyzed, most of the reported incidents related to problems with voter registration. Almost 50 percent of precincts reporting problems had a voter registration problem, nearly one-third reported some sort of problem with the poll workers, and over a quarter had some type of other administrative problem. But almost 4 of every 10 precincts reporting a problem listed something regarding their voting machines as the problem. The study also found a linkage between precincts that reported poll worker problems – such as not being fully staffed – and higher numbers of other problems reported. Some problems seem to lead to other problems.

Incident reports like these can be used in many ways to study the performance of election systems. For example, Kiewiet et al. (2008, 124–125) used these incident reports to examine whether the reported incidents had any clear partisan consequences across the county during the primary election. They found that "Democratic precincts [precincts with high voting rates for Democrats in the primary election] were more likely to report higher frequencies of problems involving poll workers.... Republican precincts, in contrast, were more likely to report incidents involving voter registration errors and encoder/access cards." Incident reports could also be integrated with voter and poll worker survey data, residual vote information, and direct election observations to provide a more comprehensive and complete portrait of the performance of an election process as well as helping to provide necessary information about potential reforms.

---

[9] Details of this analysis are available in the ESI study and in another subsequent analysis of these data by Kiewiet et al. (2008). The analysis that we discuss in this chapter is drawn from the latter source.

The incident report data from Cuyahoga County also suggest that there are certain key questions that can be asked as incident metrics that could be easily captured on a form and then scanned after the election using the same technology that is used for voting. A simple incident report form might ask a series of simple questions regarding staffing (were all the workers there and were there any worker problems?), machine issues, voter registration problems, opening and closing problems, and missing supplies. A form might also allow for open-ended responses to elaborate on the specific problems such as the nature of the voter registration problem or the type of machine issues encountered. Precincts that report problems could then be examined more carefully to determine what the causes of the problems were.[10]

Voter Registration Databases

Since the passage of HAVA in 2002, an important but relatively quiet change has taken place in most states and counties throughout the United States: the implementation of statewide, computerized voter registration systems. A decade ago, statewide computerized and electronic voter databases were not the norm in the United States, but they are the norm today.[11] Voter registration databases are used to support many of the basic functions of election administration and can produce important evaluative information and metrics that can be used to understand election system performance.

For a jurisdiction to conduct an election, an efficient and effective voter registration process is critical. The voter registration database tells election officials where voters are located, and these data are critical for election management. These data are used to determine where to locate Election Day and early voting polling places and to distribute other resources. For example, a precinct with many early and absentee

---

[10] An interesting finding of the Cuyahoga incident reports was that a very small thing – missing "I Voted" stickers – caused a very large headache at some precincts because voters want and expect this small token after they vote. Thus the incident data help illustrate some small aspects regarding what voters expect in the electoral process.

[11] The question of what constitutes a statewide database is not something we discuss in depth here, but some statewide databases are merely means of linking county-level databases into a network; other states have true statewide databases that distribute information to counties. Obviously, in either case, there are performance-based management activities that could be done at the state level with these systems.

voters may need slightly fewer staff on Election Day compared to a precinct with very low early and absentee voting. It also is important for developing ballot styles (the candidates listed on a given ballot, which vary quite a bit when there are many local races on a ballot) and for communicating with voters information about the upcoming elections. The voter registration system provides critical authentication and eligibility information for polling place operations and is used by many stakeholders for their voter mobilization and election campaigns.

The difficulty for election officials in maintaining an accurate, up-to-date voter registration system is twofold. First, the United States has a historically high rate of residential mobility.[12] Furthermore, certain segments of the electorate are more likely than others to be residentially mobile such as young voters. This makes the task of ensuring that a voter registration database is accurate and up to date an important aspect of election administration. Given this, how can election officials evaluate the performance of the voter registration system, in particular, as part of their routine administrative use of their database? And how can that information be used to better understand other aspects of election performance?

A recent study by Ansolabehere et al. (2010) used voter registration data from Los Angeles County and Florida to draw randomly selected samples of registered voters. Those selected for inclusion in the study were sent two pieces of first-class mail, both of which contained a short survey questionnaire and a return envelope. This simple but effective approach found that 5 percent of the mail was undeliverable in Los Angeles County and that 9 percent of it was undeliverable in Florida. A similar study in 2006 in one congressional district in New Mexico and Colorado found much higher rates of returned mail, with 24 percent for New Mexico and 18 percent for Colorado (Atkeson 2007a, 2007b), suggesting that the degree of problems with voter registration databases may be much higher.[13] Furthermore,

---

[12] As the CPS data show, since the collapse of the housing market in the late 2000s, U.S. migration rates have changed dramatically. Since 2005, the number of between-state moves has fallen by 3 million, and the number of cross-county, intrastate moves has declined by 1.5 million.

[13] This study included inactive voters, who by definition were already unreachable at their current addresses. However, even when these voters were removed from the survey, a 2008 New Mexico study showed that the return rate was 12%, remaining substantially high (Atkeson and Adams 2010).

in Ansolabehere's study, voters in the survey questionnaire were asked to check the accuracy of the information contained in their voter registration record; many different types of inaccuracies were revealed as part of this study.[14]

This approach could be used by election officials, especially in jurisdictions where they routinely send voting materials by postal mail. For example, in such jurisdictions, some of the mail could be sent in a way that would require return of undeliverable mail, or some of the mailings could include the same type of questionnaire, asking the recipients to verify the accuracy of their voter registration record. Not only could this information provide important data regarding the accuracy of the voter registration database, if done in advance of an election, it could help election officials allocate provisional ballot materials or determine areas of their jurisdiction where they may wish to provide refresher materials to poll workers regarding provisional balloting procedures. Data like these could also be integrated after an election with incident reports or poll worker surveys, to gauge whether problems with the registration database affected Election Day or early voting operations. New Mexico, for example, is required to send out a state mailing to all voters to determine whether an address is correct. Incorrect mailing addresses are returned to the secretary of state's office, and those voters are marked inactive. To correct these errors, the secretary attempts to match addresses with U.S. Postal Service address change information and encourages poll workers in training to request voters identified as inactive in early and Election Day voting to fill out a new voter registration form.

In another recent study, Alvarez et al. (2009c) reported on a pilot project conducted in Oregon and Washington; a pre-2008 election comparison of voter registration files across the states produced indications of thousands of instances in which voters were potentially registered to vote in the two states.[15] Not surprisingly, initial analysis of the potential duplicates between the states revealed that many were in counties along the border between the two states; procedures that

---

[14] See Ansolabehere et al. (2010) for the data on undeliverable mail. The authors discuss the results of their survey in their report "Voter Registration List Quality Pilot Studies: Report on Detailed Results" (http://vote.caltech.edu/drupal/files/report/voter_registration_list_results_pdf_4c34b18160.pdf).

[15] Alvarez et al. (2009c).

the election officials used in the two states to contact those voters who were potential duplicates produced a high response rate and thus led to some improvement in the overall accuracy of the voter registration data in the two states. List accuracy is an obvious metric for evaluating election administration performance.

Lost Votes and Metrics for Policy Change

Prior to the 2000 presidential election, few people had ever heard of a provisional ballot. But the 2000 election, and the voting problems seen in many states, brought this once obscure administrative procedure to the forefront of the debates about election reform after the 2000 presidential election. In the early days of the VTP, it searched for methods other than residual votes by which to assess performance successes – and failures – of the existing election administration system. In particular, the VTP looked for metrics that could help assess the extent to which the other aspects of the voting process – for example, voter registration and polling place problems – were leading some voters to have trouble when they went to the polls on Election Day.

Fortunately, there are systematic data that track voter registration and voting problems in federal elections that can be used to study some election problems: the U.S. Census Bureau's Current Population Survey Voting Supplement (CPS). The CPS is a survey conducted every month, but in November of every even-numbered year, the CPS includes a handful of questions about voting and the voting experience. The CPS questions are especially valuable because they are a part of a very large population sample of approximately 50,000 households. This large population allows for researchers to conduct national and state-level analyses as well as detailed demographic analysis such as experiences based on race or income. The CPS Voting Supplement has been used for important research that links state and local procedures to voter turnout. For example, the seminal research of Rosenstone and Wolfinger (1978), which identified the costs to voting associated with various voter registration requirements across states, used this data source.

Importantly, the CPS Voting Supplement asks eligible citizens if they voted, and if they say they did not vote, it asks if they were registered. Registered nonvoters are then asked, "What was the main reason you

TABLE 2.2. *Reasons for Not Voting, 2000 Presidential Election, in Percentages*

Reason	Percentage
Too busy	20.9
Illness or emergency	14.8
Not interested	12.2
Out of town	10.2
Other reasons	10.2
Didn't like the candidates	7.7
Refused, don't know	7.5
Registration problems	6.9
Forgot	4.0
Inconvenient	2.6
Transportation problems	2.4
Bad weather	0.6

did not vote?" and they are given the opportunity to provide a single answer from a long list of reasons for not voting. Table 2.2 gives the results for this question for the 2000 presidential election.[16]

Many of the reasons for not voting, while interesting, are not ones that local election officials (LEOs) or policy makers can easily resolve through changes in policy or technology. For example, 12.2 percent were not interested in the election, and 7.7 percent did not like the candidates. However, some of these responses are very important for election administrators and provide metrics for evaluating the performance of the electoral process. For example, 6.9 percent of registered nonvoters said they did not vote because they had a registration problem. The CPS estimates that there were approximately 43 million registered nonvoters in 2000.[17] If 6.9 percent of them could not vote due to registration problems, that is nearly 3 million lost votes due to voter registration problems alone. The exact nature of these voter registration problems is not clear from these data – the CPS questionnaire does not follow up with these respondents as to what the problem was – but it is likely that some combination of problems associated

[16] Jamieson et al. (2002, 10).

[17] The Federal Election Commission found that the states reported 149,476,705 active registered voters in 2000 (FEC n.d., 1). The turnout estimate (107,390,107) is from Michael McDonald's "General Election Turnout Rate" database, http://elections.gmu.edu/Turnout_2000G.html.

with errors in voter registration lists, incomplete or inaccurate voter registration information, or other voter registration mix-ups produces these problems.

Data like the CPS Voting Supplement, in combination with residual vote estimates, allowed the VTP to produce some overall estimates of election performance in the form of lost votes measures. In particular, the VTP estimated that between 1.5 and 2 million votes were lost due to bad ballots and faulty voting machines; between 1.5 and 3 million votes were lost due to voter registration problems; approximately 1 million votes were lost due to problems in polling places; and an unknown number were lost due to problems with absentee ballots. These estimates were important guides for policy makers who worked at both the state and federal levels on election reforms after the 2000 presidential election.

We will have much more to say about voter evaluations and survey methodologies later in the book, but the important issue here is that by using this methodology – and using some very simple metrics based on available data – the VTP team was able to make policy recommendations to address the problem. Specifically, most of the votes lost because of voter registration problems could likely be recovered if those states that did not allow for a provisional voting procedure (about half of the states in 2000) developed one and if the rest of the states more aggressively used their existing provisional ballot procedures. This argument was reflected in the HAVA, which, when passed in 2002, required that states develop and implement a provisional voting procedure or an equivalent alternative policy.

Moving from Data to Performance-Based Management

Although election officials normally collect a wealth of data in their election processes, most of the data go into one report: the election canvass. In this report, the election officials report aggregate totals of ballots cast and counted and, in some cases, turnout. For many election jurisdictions, the completion of this report and its approval by the governmental canvass board (and subsequent acceptance by the chief state election officer) are the proof that the election was conducted successfully. However, what this report does not provide are metrics regarding the performance of the electoral system. A canvass report is a one-off event and, without comparable data across elections, election management and performance measurement, too, are often treated as one-off occurrences. The question at a canvass is often "Was *this* election successful in that we have definitive winners in the races?" instead of "How did this election compare to past elections across all of our performance measures?"

The latter question brings us back to the issue with which we started the book: improving elections through an effective performance-based management process. As defined by the Government Accountability Office – the flagship organization in government for audit and evaluation – performance-based management is

the ongoing monitoring and reporting of program accomplishments, particularly progress towards preestablished goals. It is typically conducted by program or agency management. Performance measures may address the type or level of program activities conducted (process), the direct products and services delivered by a program (outputs), and/or the results of those products and services (outcomes).[18]

What is necessary for effective performance-based management is a system that can identify outcomes but also help to identify why those outcomes occurred. As Hatry (1999) notes, a manager needs to know the score of the game (the outcome measures) but also how the points were scored (input, output, and related outcome data). Hatry identifies eight categories of information for performance-based management, as shown in Table 2.3. We have added a second column to this table, providing an example of what such a measure would be in election administration performance measurement and management.

To evaluate and measure performance in election administration, election officials need to start by identifying key inputs, processes, outputs, and outcomes and then design measures for determining how well the organization is addressing these issues. If we consider these issues in reverse order, outcome measures based on regularly collected data might include the following categories:

---

[18] GAO, "Performance Measurement and Evaluation: Definitions and Relationships," May 2005, http://www.gao.gov/new.items/d05739sp.pdf.

TABLE 2.3. *Performance-Based Management and Elections*

Category of Information	Example
Inputs	Number of ballots printed; number of poll workers; number of voter information cards mailed out
Processes	Volume of absentee ballot processes per day
Outputs	Number of voters processed
Outcomes	
Intermediate outcomes	Voter confidence; voter satisfaction with poll workers
Final outcomes	Residual vote rates
Efficiency/productivity	Cost per vote cast (by vote mode); votes cast per poll worker (by precinct)
Workload and demographic information	Voter satisfaction by race, age, party, or voting mode; workload across vote mode
Explanatory information	Budget data; type of election (presidential vs. local only)
Impacts	Voting services that lower costs of voting and increase turnout or satisfaction

Residual vote rates. These can be measured via computing the rate of residual votes for each voting mode (early, Election Day, and absentee) and for special populations of voters such as overseas military and civilian voters. A lower rate – and similarly low rates across modes – would be one piece of evidence supporting the conclusion that it was a well-run election. Likewise, a higher rate within a particular mode, for example among absentee voters, may suggest a voter education problem.

Turnout. In thinking about election outcomes, the election officials should not consider turnout as an independent outcome because, in general, turnout is driven by factors outside their control such as party mobilization activities and weather (Green and Gerber 2008; Gomez, Hansford and Krause 2007). However, turnout may be an indicator of problems with outcomes or processes, such as absentee processes, as discussed later.

When considering outcome measures, the following are examples of what can be measured and how they can provide feedback on the quality of this election and places for improvement in the next election. In the language of audits, we can think of these as audit findings that would have proposed corrective actions, which is what are needed for improvement in performance over time.

Absentee ballot mailing and return. Election officials can track in their voter file (1) the date on which absentee ballots were requested, (2) the date the requested ballot was mailed, (3) the date a ballot was returned, and (4) the number of unreturned ballots. These data will allow election officials to identify what type of voter is requesting absentee ballots, the type of voter not returning ballots (or returning them late), and which precincts are being more or less affected by absentee voting rates. High unreturned rates may indicate problems with the U.S. Postal Service or with other mailing processes.

Absentee ballot rejections. One key issue with the move toward convenience voting is that absentee voting provides more possibilities for the voter to have a problem with the ballot that results in the entire ballot not being counted. Election officials can track the reason why ballots are not counted – no signature on the envelope, returned late – and try to determine what procedurally is leading to this outcome. Such actions might lead to clearer instructions and better voter education.

Provisional ballot rejections and rates. The rate of provisional balloting can be informative if the election officials capture the reason for the provisional ballot being cast. Provisional voting can be a function of voter registration system problems, problems locating polling locations, problems with unregistered voters wanting to vote, or voter identification issues. Knowing the rate and reason for provisional ballots is important for determining if there is a process problem.

One provisional ballot disposition that is particularly informative is provisional ballot rejections. For example, if provisional ballots are being rejected because either voters or poll workers are not completing the outer envelope correctly, that is important information regarding where better training of poll workers should be a focus.

Early voting rates. Rates of early voting are important as an outcome measure because this measure, in turn, is an input measure into the number of voters who will be eligible to vote by precinct or vote center on Election Day. Between early voting, absentee voting rates, and previous turnout history, election officials can better predict what precincts will likely be busier on Election Day and allocate staff resources accordingly.

When considering process measures, the following are examples of what can be measured:

Polling place problems. Poll workers log data and data from election "rovers" from the central election office can both provide metrics regarding problems with polling places, including accessibility, visibility, and parking. These data can be used to identify low-quality precincts so that they could be replaced by new facilities in the future.

Procedural completion success. When considering Election Day voting especially, there are numerous procedural benchmarks that can be evaluated, using data that are captured for other reasons. These include (1) the time the optical scan tabulator or direct recording electronic (DRE) machines were started, (2) the correctness of the end-of-night ballot reconciliation forms, (3) the correctness of forms documenting the sealing of ballots and machines, and (4) the correctness of all machine closeouts. These documents allow election officials to see where procedural breakdowns occurred, which can feed back into training priorities. Typically, these data are included in the logs that voting machines produce.

Problems in voting. There are also data that can be identified regarding voter problems with voting technologies. These include (1) the number of spoiled paper ballots per precinct and (2) the number of DRE voters who reviewed their ballot and then corrected their vote. The former are typically collected as a part of election canvasses but not analyzed in the way we are considering here. The latter data can be collected based on the way data are logged by voting machine vendors.

Input data are more obvious here and include factors like the number of ballots printed, the number of polling places operated (Election Day and early), the number of poll workers hired, and the number of voter information cards sent out.

In the next several chapters, we will discuss several other key performance measures that can be collected by election officials if they are able to do so. These measures can add an important level of depth and richness to measurement of election performance. Key indicators include the following:

Voter feedback. This can be measured through voter surveys, which can ask about (1) confidence that votes will be counted accurately; (2)

the quality of voter–poll worker interactions; (3) ease of absentee voting instructions; (4) wait times for in-person voting; (5) the consistency with which procedures are applied, such as voter identification, across voters; and so on.

Poll worker feedback. This can be measured through poll worker surveys, which can ask about (1) confidence that they were well prepared on Election Day, (2) confidence that votes were counted accurately, (3) assessment of the quality of the training, (4) identification of particular procedural problems such as reconciliation, (5) the consistency with which policies are implemented such as voter identification, (6) the quality of precincts, (7) the adequacy of the supplies, (8) their desire to work in the next election, and so on.

Using Performance Data for Election Improvement

So an election official has these data collected and in a data set. What should be done with them? First and foremost, the data should be reported in the lowest aggregation possible, which in most election environments would be at the precinct level. With this information, it is possible to do several important management activities.

Benchmarking. For each indicator, it is possible to determine what the median or average was for the jurisdiction and then identify which precincts are above or below the median. These initial values also serve as a benchmark for identifying future performance in the jurisdiction and in each precinct. Thus precincts can be compared within the same election and across similar election contexts to look for changes in patterns. Benchmarks for absolute performance, such as having no more than one precinct per election opening more than five minutes late, are another form of benchmark that tests performance against an ideal standard. Both types of benchmarks are important for performance measurement and improvement.

Evaluation of outcomes. Data on precinct performance can be merged with other data about that precinct such as Census demographic information or demographic information from the voter registration files such as the data on the percentage of voters who voted by vote mode, or poll worker and voter survey data, to determine what factors may have affected the outcome in that precinct. The reason for pursuing an ecological approach is to ensure that there are the best data possible for identifying the factors causing certain outcomes and that performance is measured completely.

Conclusions

Election officials – as well as stakeholders and researchers – all are interested in determining ways to improve election administration. However, doing this requires collecting data systematically and making sure that all of the important evaluative data have been identified. Of course, we know that developing and deploying many of these methods will require financial, personnel, and other logistical resources, and in today's economic times (and even in the best economic times!), resources for such studies are often quite limited.

That is why we have provided four examples in this chapter of evaluative data that are often routinely collected by election officials or that could be collected in the future at little additional cost. In our discussion of these examples, we have shown how these data have been used to better understand the performance of election administration in the past – and we have also pointed out ways in which they could be used in the future to even better assess the performance of election administration.

It does not stretch the imagination – nor potentially strain the budget of a state or county – to see how a jurisdiction could ensure it collects and publishes performance measurement data that would allow for computation of residual votes, collects and publishes data on provisional balloting, works with polling place workers to collect feedback and incident reports, and works to utilize its voter registration databases to assess its performance. These data can be collected by the jurisdiction itself or working in collaboration with local researchers or stakeholders who might have additional resources for such analysis. The jurisdiction – either by itself or with outside assistance – can use these readily available data to evaluate multiple aspects of each election in the jurisdiction and to develop strong baseline data that can be used to understand how administrative or technological innovations either serve to improve or hinder election performance.

Most important, the data from these performance measurement activities can be used to improve elections in a jurisdiction systematically. The training, procedures, and practices for elections can be adjusted based on the findings of these analyses, and successes can be emphasized. Moreover, the systematic collection of data can allow election administrators to make clearer claims on resources and to make requests for policy changes from their counties or from their state legislatures.

3

Measuring the Experiences of Voters

In today's business world, measurement of the quality of the consumer's experience is essential. Businesses, especially those in areas like retail, spend untold sums of money researching what their consumers want, how they enjoy their shopping experiences, and what new products and services they may want. Think about all the times you have made an online purchase of a product or service and, at the end, you get a request to complete a short survey. In today's busy marketplace, where individuals have many potential outlets for their purchases, corporations are always studying what they can do to make each transaction better.

Although such consumer-oriented research is ubiquitous in the private sector, such tools have not been largely adopted by government entities.[1] This is particularly true for election administrators, who rarely try to obtain systematic feedback from those who are the primary consumers of their services: voters. The other key stakeholders of the services of election officials include candidates running for office, political parties, and voter advocacy groups. Because these groups are generally well-organized, formal entities, they often have structured methods of providing feedback to election officials about the quality

[1] One reason why this is not the case is because of normative concerns about whether public-sector government of citizens' transactions should be viewed as using this market-based lens of "customer service"; see, e.g., Kelly (2005, 76–84) for a discussion of this point.

of the election-related services they received and the performance of their administrative practices.[2]

We argue in this chapter that it is imperative that election officials, and others who are interested in determining the performance of election administration, study in a systematic fashion the experiences, perceptions, and opinions of voters. A wealth of performance metrics can be developed from these surveys, as we will note. Fortunately, this is an area where there is much that social scientists can offer to the study of election administration performance; methods for studying the evaluations, opinions, and perceptions of individuals have been well studied in the social sciences for decades. This chapter presents a variety of methods that can be used by election officials to understand the experiences of their primary consumers and gives examples from our own research.

These methods fall into two basic types: qualitative and quantitative. Qualitative data of individual opinions and perceptions are often collected in focus groups. These are really conversations that go on between a facilitator and a small group of selected individuals, where the facilitator seeks to guide the conversation to cover certain topics. Such qualitative studies are frequently used by market researchers when they wish to really understand in detail the reactions of selected types of individuals to new products as a well-trained and well-prepared facilitator can go into great and productive detail about certain topics. They are also helpful in other situations, especially when the researcher does not know well what opinions people might have or what their general knowledge is about a certain subject.

Qualitative research like this is, in many cases, highly productive, but such studies are not necessarily reflective of the opinions and evaluations of the general population. Thus great care must be taken when one interprets the results from a focus group research project, as their

---

[2] An excellent example of such mechanisms for stakeholder feedback is the Community Voter Outreach Committee, sponsored by the Los Angeles Registrar/Recorder County Clerk (http://www.lavote.net/Voter/CVOC/Default.cfm). This is a committee sponsored by the Registrar/Recorder's office; it meets regularly, and it has a broad and diverse membership. To the extent that the members represent the breadth and diversity of the electorate in Los Angeles County, this can be seen as a means of gathering voter feedback, but it is much more indirect and much less systematic than the approaches we discuss in this chapter. See Hall (2003).

small size means that the conversations that go on in these groups may not be representative of the broader population. Also, as these conversations are led by a facilitator, and are conversations between group members, their results can be highly susceptible to how the conversation is framed and how the issues are discussed.[3]

For these very reasons, market researchers will often team their focus group research with a survey study, where a survey is taken of a larger and more scientifically sampled group of individuals from the population. Although survey research is based on a number of important assumptions, and can be poorly implemented, if it is done well, much can be learned about the opinions, evaluations, and perceptions of the population from which the survey respondents are drawn.

Qualitative Methods and the Voting Experience

Focus groups are widely used in market research. If a private business is bringing a new food product to market, making a new video game, producing a new movie, or developing a new television advertising campaign, companies will typically utilize some type of focus group research in the early stages of that marketing effort to determine if their efforts are correctly focused. Focus group studies are also widely used in the political arena, typically by candidates and campaigns when they are trying to develop their messages. In our experience, political groups will convene focus groups very early in the campaign to assess a wide range of reactions to the candidate, to her opponent, and to a broad range of methods that might be used in positive and negative ways to win a particular election. Pending available resources, political campaigns will often develop a message and then later test it in rounds of focus group research.

However, in our research on election administration, we have rarely heard of the widespread use of systematic focus group research, especially aimed at understanding the current experiences of voters or to test new methods of administering an election or voting. We surmise that this is not because election officials do not want to learn about voter experiences or about better means of marketing their services

---

[3] E.g., focus groups can become dominated by an individual who can shape the conversation in a way that would not be reflective of the population.

to voters but instead is due to a lack of resources and understanding about how these methods can be used effectively.

An Example: The Voting Systems Assessment Project

The Voting Systems Assessment Project (VSAP) is a recent research effort by the Caltech/MIT Voting Technology Project. This effort seeks to help Los Angeles County, the nation's largest and most diverse election jurisdiction, as it moves to determine what sort of voting system(s) are most appropriate for acquisition in the near future. Los Angeles County was one of the jurisdictions that used the now infamous Votomatic punch card voting system, until it was decertified in the aftermath of the 2000 presidential election. After the decertification, Los Angeles County lacked the necessary resources to undertake the acquisition of a new voting system and also faced a very uncertain regulatory environment in California that made purchasing a new system potentially risky (any new system might be decertified in such an environment). In the meantime, the county has relied on an interim voting system, InkaVote, which utilizes a ballot and underlying technology that are quite similar to the previous punch card voting system. Instead of punching out the chad, the voter bubbles in the chad, and it is then scanned.

The first stage of research for the VSAP involved the development of multiple mechanisms for public engagement; one of the primary methods of public engagement used in the VSAP was a series of focus group studies conducted in April and May 2010. A total of 12 focus groups were convened during this period, each designed to facilitate the input from diverse groups of Los Angeles County voters, especially from groups that might not be well represented in a more traditional survey study. Specifically, the focus group research effort targeted groups of registered Los Angeles County voters who represent the diversity of the Los Angeles voting population as well as key groups who are most likely to be sensitive to questions of usability with the voting system. These groups included:

- two groups of all general electorate voters
- one group of permanent vote-by-mail
- one group of African Americans
- one group of young (18- to 25-year-old) voters

- two groups of Latino registered voters (one English speaking, one Spanish speaking)
- two groups of voters with disabilities
- three groups of Asian voters (one English speaking, one Korean speaking, and one Mandarin speaking)

Each focus group involved approximately 8 to 10 participants (the groups with disabled voters were somewhat larger so as to better represent the diversity of disabilities). The groups were recruited by a professional qualitative research firm in Los Angeles, and all the sessions were conducted at this firm's Los Angeles research facility.[4]

These focus groups were conducted to better understand the experience of voters in Los Angeles County: why they participate in voting, whether they have had problems when they tried to vote in the past, their views on the InkaVote system, their opinions about possible new voting systems, their trust and confidence in the election process, and finally, how they think new voting systems should be developed and maintained.

To frame the rest of the focus group discussion, the focus moderator began a discussion of the experiences of participants the last time they voted. In each case, this introduction led to a good discussion of the things that participants did and did not like about the voting process in recent years. The moderator then shifted the discussion to a general evaluation of how elections are conducted in both the United States and in Los Angeles County. This general introduction is typical for focus group studies. Discussions of general experiences and opinions tend to break the ice in small groups and also help to get participants thinking about elections and their experiences voting, which, of course, is the point of this particular project.

The focus groups then moved into the heart of the discussion, with the moderator passing out a piece of paper and asking participants to write down three things they did and did not like about the

---

[4] Of course, how a focus group study is implemented will be determined largely by available resources. If possible, utilizing a professional research firm reduces the logistical complexities of undertaking a focus group research study, and it also helps to ensure that participants understand the neutrality of the research effort. Focus group members are typically paid for their time with a small stipend and are recruited from the voter registration rolls.

voting process in Los Angeles County. The written exercise is helpful as it forces participants to develop a response prior to hearing
the opinions and evaluations of other participants. It also provides
a written record that researchers can use to document the participants' opinions after the group is finished. Participants were then asked
to discuss their evaluations, to talk about how they got information
about the voting process, to elaborate on what happens to their ballot
after it is cast, and to talk about whether they are confident in the
process.

Then the focus group discussions moved to one of the most important research questions: a discussion of the most important aspects
of a voting system. The dimensions of the voting system that were of
most importance for our discussion were those related to security, cost
effectiveness, ease of use, reliability, auditability, speed and accuracy
of counting, speed of voting, verification of votes, and privacy. Participants were asked to rank the most important of these aspects, and
in each of the focus groups sessions, there was a lengthy discussion of
these various priorities.

Next, the moderator led the participants through a mock voting
exercise using the existing voting systems in Los Angeles County and
then asked them to evaluate the voting process they used relative to
the voting system priorities they just discussed. Afterward, the groups
discussed alternative voting systems such as optical scanning or other
types of computerized voting procedures. Finally, the groups discussed
who should develop and maintain new voting systems in Los Angeles
County: private entities, the county, or some combination of the two.

A number of members of the VSAP research project observed each
focus group session, and they took detailed notes and observations.
The group sessions were recorded, and transcripts of those recordings
were provided to the research team. The accumulated information was
then used to produce a preliminary report.

Some of these findings were quite important. For example, generally
speaking, the focus group participants articulated a very high degree
of trust and confidence in the election process in Los Angeles County,
and they typically expressed few problems with the existing voting
process. Furthermore, as they evaluated voting systems, most participants would typically discuss the importance of security, accuracy,
convenience, and ease of use. These basic findings were seen by the

VSAP research team as some of the most important ones to arise out of this focus group study.

In this case, we represented groups of voters through their systematic identification within the voter file, but election officials could do similar projects to obtain feedback from particular segments or the general population of voters. For example, local election officials could be in touch with groups, such as the League of Women Voters, advocates for individuals with disabilities, or groups that focus on youth or minority voters, to identify key people to participate in such an activity. But the most important aspect of this process is that the data it provides are looked at systematically and that the process is there to feed back into the improvement loop in the election process.

Reviewing the work of the VSAP, focus group research can be used to create several important metrics in elections. The most important metric concerns the opinions of groups who are most vulnerable to problems with the electoral process such as older voters, individuals with disabilities, language minority voters, and voters who vote in a special way (such as permanent absentee voters or military and overseas voters).

Quantitative Performance Measurement Metrics

For election officials, the voter might be considered the most important constituent – or, in the language of business, the most important customer segment. By measuring voter experiences, election officials have data that they can use to evaluate the performance of their organizations, as perceived by the voter. Election officials want to run elections that are free of problems, leave voters confident with the result of the voting process, and give positive customer service experience with the frontline election workers (the poll workers for in-person voters).

One key way of studying the experiences of voters is through large-scale surveys, as are done every day by survey research firms for public and private clients. Prior to the 2000 presidential election, there were few large-scale efforts undertaken to study voter experiences using traditional survey methods. Instead, election surveys, such as the American National Election Study or the National Annenberg Election Survey, have always asked about the campaign, information about political attitudes, and vote choice; little content was included about the voting experience itself.[5] The only significant exception to this that we know of is the example we discussed earlier, the U.S. Census Bureau's Current Population Study (CPS) Voting Supplement. This set of questions added to the monthly CPS in November of every even year asks registered voters why they didn't participate and unregistered voters why they are not registered. In the last decade, it has added questions regarding how people have cast their ballots in response to changes in the way people vote, with the expansion in use of early and absentee voting.

The data from the CPS have proven to be invaluable for the study of voting participation in the United States. Because of the very large sample size of the survey, it is possible to make state-level estimates of the factors that affect voter registration rates and voter turnout. In fact, two metrics – for evaluating states, not localities – can be derived easily from the CPS data:

- CPS data can be used to examine barriers to registering to vote. Some of the first policy work on voter registration laws was conducted in the 1970s using CPS data to determine which barriers in state law made it hard for individuals to register – and stay registered – to vote (Rosenstone and Wolfinger 1978).
- CPS data were used by the VTP to estimate many dimensions of lost votes in the 2000 presidential election, based on voters being unable to vote because of problems registering, problems voting, and other problems at the polls.

Even though the CPS is a valuable data source, it does not provide the sort of detailed information one might need to really understand how elections are conducted in geographic units smaller than states. The CPS also focuses solely on registration and voting; it neither asks about the voting experience nor provides a wealth of important variables that have been shown to be important in research such as partisan affiliation and voter confidence. To conduct the type of voter-centered survey that can be used for performance measurement, local election officials or scholars working with them need to design surveys

---

[5] With the one exception of the 1976 American National Election Study, which, as part of its vote validation study, included an election administration component. See http://electionstudies.org/studypages/1976prepost/1976prepost.htm.

that assess the voting experience specific to that jurisdiction. In the appendix to this chapter, we discuss a variety of approaches for the implementation of voter surveys that will provide detailed information about the voting experience. Here we present a number of examples from our own research, where we have implemented such survey studies.

Survey of the Performance of American Elections

One example of the use of surveys for studying voter experiences in elections is the Survey of the Performance of American Elections (SPAE). First conducted in 2007, and conducted twice more in 2008 and once in 2009, the SPAE surveyed voters about numerous performance metrics and questions related to election administration. Reviewing the questions asked in these surveys can illustrate the types of questions that can be used by election officials as performance measurement metrics for evaluating their organizations and their elections.

These surveys asked about both modes of voting in the United States. Voters can vote (1) in person on Election Day at a local precinct or before Election Day at an early voting location or (2) remotely, using a paper ballot that is mailed back to the election official.[6] For the in-person evaluation, these surveys asked about the following metrics:

- How easy was it to find the polling place?
- How well run was the polling place?
- Were there problems at the polling place that could have interfered with people being able to vote?
- Did the voter experience a voter registration problem?
- Did the voter experience a problem with the voting equipment?
- How long did the voter wait in line to vote?
- Did the voter feel that her vote was cast in an environment that was private?
- Did the voter feel intimidated in any way during the casting of her vote?

---

[6] Some jurisdictions are allowing Internet voting for military or overseas voters, as part of pilot projects, and they can be evaluated in a way similar to the way in which absentee voters are surveyed, albeit with questions tailored for the technological interaction that Internet voting affords.

- Was the voter asked to present photo identification at the polls before voting and, if so, did she do so because she was asked or on her own initiative?

The importance of these questions is that they provide a multilayered view of the in-person voting process. They ask about an array of steps in the voting process and try to discern whether problems occurred at any step. These questions all also feed into two important summary judgment questions that can be used to evaluate voters' confidence in key aspects of the election:

- How would the voter evaluate the performance of the poll worker?
- How confident is the voter that her ballot was counted accurately?

Several studies have found that questions like these provide an overall summary evaluation of the voter's experience (Alvarez et al. 2007a; Atkeson and Saunders 2007; Hall and Stewart 2011). Problems in the voting process tend to be reflected in the evaluation that voters have of poll workers, who should have ensured that the problems did not occur, and in evaluations of voter confidence, as the voter may not be sure that the vote was counted accurately because of the problems that arose.

For the absentee voting process, a similar set of metrics was asked. These included the following:

- Did the voter have a problem getting the ballot?
- Did the voter need assistance completing the absentee ballot?
- Did the voter feel pressured to vote a particular way when completing the absentee ballot (i.e., was the voter subject to intimidation)?
- How easy was it to follow all the instructions necessary to cast and return the absentee ballot?
- When did the voter return the absentee ballot?
- How confident is the voter that her absentee ballot was counted?

Again, these metrics provide important information about the performance of the absentee voting process. The election official can learn about issues voters may be having in getting ballots on time, finding voting to be an easy process, and feeling confident that their ballots are being counted.

The VSAP Example

In the VSAP, a large sample of registered voters, more than 1,000 in total, were surveyed using both an Internet survey and a telephone survey (more about the methodology for this survey can be found in the appendix to this chapter). Given the ethnic diversity of Los Angeles, the research team also fielded the survey in both Spanish and Mandarin Chinese. The survey also included some cellular telephone users, which is becoming the sole method of telephone contact for many Americans (Blumberg and Luke 2011). The VSAP survey used questions that had been fielded on earlier surveys, which helped to ensure that the questions were valid and gave responses that would be useful (Alvarez et al. 2009a; Atkeson 2007a, 2007b). These considerations led to the following mixed-mode implementation: a total of 651 interviews were completed by telephone, including 25 Mandarin Chinese respondents, 51 Spanish respondents, and 80 cell phone respondents. Five hundred interviews were done online.

The results of the VSAP surveys found that, overall, most Los Angeles County voters, without information to the contrary, did not think that the existing InkaVote system should be replaced. Only 21 percent of the telephone sample and 14 percent of the Internet sample said it should be replaced. But the survey also found that these opinions might be malleable; registered voters in the sample were also asked which kind of voting system they would most prefer to vote on. In both samples, a plurality of respondents said that they would prefer to vote on an electronic voting machine (43% in the telephone sample and 28% in the Internet sample). The VSAP surveys also asked the registered voters in the sample about what attributes they valued in a voting system – respondents were asked to rank their first and second priorities from a long list. In both samples, accurately counting votes was ranked first by the most respondents, followed by security. The respondents in each sample were then most likely to rank either reliability or ease of use as the next set of priorities.

What is quite important about the VSAP survey is that it was closely integrated with the focus group study. The two in combination allowed the research team to be confident about some of the inferences they drew from both studies. Given that the focus group and survey approaches used very different methodologies, when they yielded results that were in agreement, this allowed the research team to be more confident in their inferences and conclusions.

Note, for example, that the survey and focus group studies produced results that indicated that similar voting system priorities were important to voters in Los Angeles County: accuracy, security, reliability, and ease of use. Given that focus group participants and survey respondents typically agreed on the ordering of these priorities, the research team could be quite confident that these likely reflect the overall state of opinion about voting system values in Los Angeles County. This information helped to inform the efforts of election officials as they explored public opinion on desirable voting machines to replace the existing voting system in Los Angeles County.

The New Mexico 2006–2010 Voter Surveys

A different example of how to conduct a voter evaluation survey comes from other recent research that was begun in 2006 and has continued in 2008 and 2010, providing a cross-sectional time series data set on New Mexico voters. The 2006 study (Alvarez et al. 2007a; Atkeson 2007a, 2007b) represents an early attempt to access voter experiences across all types of voters (Election Day, early, and absentee) and with a wide variety of questions in a specific locality.[7] The 2006 survey focused on the First Congressional District in New Mexico (NM1), which is largely Bernalillo County. Fully 95 percent of voters in NM1 live in Bernalillo County (Atkeson and Tafoya 2008). The New Mexico secretary of state provided the statewide voter registration file to the researchers to use as the sample to randomly select a sample of potential voters for the study, with nonvoters screened out of the study.

We had the good fortune to follow up on the 2006 study in 2008 (Atkeson, Alvarez, and Hall 2010c) and continued the project in 2010 (Atkeson et al. 2011a). In the two latter elections, the project moved from predominantly one election jurisdiction to the entire state. In many ways, the New Mexico project is an example of conducting ongoing performance measurement research, as the study of elections

---

[7] The survey also includes a similar survey for Colorado's Seventh Congressional District as part of its research design.

in several counties and statewide has been done multiple times using the same metrics. The time series not only allows us to look at change over time but also allows us to form new questions based on earlier results. Thus, when problems or concerns are identified, we can expand our study next time to obtain more detail. For example, in 2008, we learned that a surprising number of voters indicated that they had witnessed election fraud. We asked, "In the last ten years, in how many elections have you witnessed what you think to be election fraud?" Over two in five (43%) of voters indicated that they had witnessed one or more fraudulent election incidents in the past 10 years. In 2010, we expanded this question with an open-ended response, giving the opportunity for respondents to describe the fraud. We found that largely, voters indicated that they saw fraud in the 2000 and 2004 elections. Thus, for many voters, witnessing fraud was not something they personally observed in their community but was something they "witnessed" or "experienced" vis-à-vis the media, nationally, and is related to national discussions framed from the 2000 and 2004 presidential elections in other states.

The study also allows us to reflect on client (poll worker and voter) support for various policies. So, for example, in 2008, the county clerks in New Mexico were interested in moving to more all-mail elections, but research showed there was little support for this change. In 2010, the county clerks were interested in moving toward vote centers instead of a precinct-based voting system, which would reduce their costs and increase their efficiency on Election Day. As part of the study, we asked both poll workers and voters to evaluate their attitudes toward changing from precinct-based voting to vote centers. As we describe at the beginning of the last section of the voter survey, "Vote centers are a polling place at which any registered voter in the county may vote. They are similar to early voting locations, placed in large buildings and offer many voting stations. Many counties and states in the nation are moving from traditional precinct voting to vote centers." To measure attitudes about centers, we asked respondents to initially place themselves on a 0–10 scale, where 0 represented no support for the move to vote centers and 10 represented strong support for the move to vote centers. Voters were then asked to consider additional arguments or statements about the strengths and weaknesses of vote centers and how each new question alters their opinion on whether

New Mexico should change from precinct voting to vote center voting on Election Day. In total, there were seven questions related to vote centers in the survey. On average, voters placed themselves toward the center of the scale, suggesting that they were somewhat ambivalent and open to this new means of voting. Importantly, the survey found that both negative and positive arguments overall increased support for vote centers by over half (.63) a point. These data helped to structure debate around the legislative question and to show that the move on average would not be disruptive to voters. Thus a data-driven approach to election reform can assist with new issues as they arise.

Metrics from Voter Surveys

As we noted at the beginning of the chapter, numerous metrics can be obtained from voter surveys. In this section, we illustrate several of these metrics, using data from surveys that have been done in Los Angeles, New Mexico, or nationally. We consider measures of voter confidence in the vote counting process, voter experiences with poll workers, problems at the polling location, wait times, and issues related to voter identification.

Voter Confidence

Voter surveys can provide several important performance metrics that are a key part of any performance measurement system for election administration. One critical metric that has been a part of many of the studies in which we have been involved is, how confident are voters in the overall electoral process? In New Mexico, Los Angeles, and SPAE, the question of confidence has been important because it provides feedback regarding the efficacy of various sweeping technological and administrative changes that have been made to the election process in the state and regarding voter confidence in the voting process.

One of the key benefits of conducting continuous measurement of key election metrics is that it is possible to make a comparison of voter confidence over time. Many of the questions from the studies in New Mexico have now been asked over three election cycles, so it is possible to compare changes in voter confidence between 2006, 2008, and 2010 in Bernalillo County and statewide between 2008 and 2010.

TABLE 3.1. *Voter Confidence over Time in Bernalillo County, New Mexico*

	2006 Voter Confidence	2008 Voter Confidence	2010 Voter Confidence
Bernalillo			
Very confident	35.9	54.4	49.2
Somewhat confident	43.9	39.7	44.2
Not very confident	10.4	4.8	4.00
Not at all confident	3.4	1.2	2.0
Mean	$3.20^{a,b}$	3.47	3.42
N	388	257	301
Statewide			
Very confident		53.3	53.6
Somewhat confident		39.3	39.5
Not too confident		5.1	5.1
Not at all confident		2.3	1.8
Mean		3.44	3.44
N		636	823

[a] Significant difference between 2006 and 2008, two-tailed test, $p < .001$.
[b] Significant difference between 2006 and 2010, two-tailed test, $p < .001$.

Table 3.1 shows data on voter confidence over time.[8] The data show that voter confidence has increased between 2006 and 2008, with nearly 15 percent more voters "very confident" and 10 percent fewer voters only somewhat or not at all confident.

From a management perspective, these data are very important because they illustrate that – on a basic level – Bernalillo County voters were more confident that their vote was counted correctly in 2010 and 2008 than in 2006. In addition, we can see that voters held the same confidence level overall in 2008 as they did in 2010. Indeed, the frequencies are extremely close.

This headline, however, does not fully answer the performance question. For example, a manager would want to know if this confidence increase held true across important subpopulations – such as by ethnic groups (in the case of New Mexico, between Hispanics and whites),

---

[8] We show only the data for the mixed-mode survey as the telephone survey was only done in 2008 and voters in this survey mode indicated higher voter confidence than those in the mixed-mode survey, where there was no interviewer (Atkeson et al. 2010a, 2010d).

across vote modes (early, absentee, and in-person Election Day voting), and across habitual voters, who vote all the time, and casual voters, who might only vote in presidential years. For example, we found that there is no difference between Hispanics and whites across all three election contexts in terms of their personal voter confidence. We found that there is some evidence that absentee voters are just slightly less confident than their in-person peers. However, we found no difference between voting modes in 2008, which suggests that there may be differences between presidential election voting experiences and those in congressional elections.

Polling Place Metrics

Wait Times

We can also compare metrics in performance, for example, the quantity of time average voters had to wait at the poll, an often considered metric of successful election administration (Alvarez et al. 2009a; Gerken 2009). We found that there is a reduction in wait time over the three years of study in Bernalillo County. Early voters indicated that on average, they waited in line 31 minutes in 2006, 16 minutes in 2008, and 6 minutes in 2010. Similarly, Election Day voters went from waiting an average of 9 minutes in 2006, to 5 minutes in 2008, to only 3 minutes in 2010. Over the same period, the local election official increased the number of early voting locations and hired more staff for Election Day activities. The data suggest that these measures are working and that more voters are being served more quickly than previously. Thus the over-time data allow us a quantitative look at how changes in operations actually influence or alter changes in behavior. In this case, the 2006 performance data suggested a problem, and management changes designed to address performance on this metric improved the individual experiences of the voters in subsequent elections.

Problems at the Polls

Voter surveys also allow for the capture of many other performance metric data that can be helpful in understanding election system performance. One important metric is the frequency of voters having problems in the voting process. The SPAE and New Mexico survey asked about several metrics related to problem voting. These included questions regarding voter registration and problems in the actual voting process such as spoiling a ballot and having to vote again; having problems understanding voting directions, especially for absentee voters; having problems finding the polling place; waiting in long lines; and having problems with the voting technology used or feeling intimidated.

Data about problems at the polls are important for several reasons. First, they provide information about the issue in question. Election officials need to know if their polling places are hard to find, if there are problems with voting machines, or if the registration lists in some precincts have many problems. Although these problems were generally found in less than 2 percent of precincts in the 2008 SPAE, these problems can be illustrative of larger process issues at a polling location. These questions can provide metrics on overall precinct performance, especially when combined into a "voter experienced problem" metric.

By using multiple metrics, it is possible to determine how changes in certain metrics affect other metrics. For example, it is logical to think that voter interactions with their ballots might be correlated with voter confidence. However, in the New Mexico case, the data showed that a voter spoiling a ballot for some reason and having to obtain a new one did not lower voter confidence. Likewise, having a problem with an absentee ballot also did not lower voter confidence. In 2008, the only factor that seemed to make a difference was whether an absentee voter thought that the instructions for filling out and returning her ballot were easy or hard to follow. Those who thought the instructions were somewhat hard were less confident than those who thought the instructions were very easy or fairly easy (Atkeson et al. 2010c). Similarly, in 2006, we found that the more a voter thought the ballot was confusing, the more it reduced her voter confidence (Atkeson and Saunders 2007). Note the importance of these findings for managers; this suggests that providing clear instructions about using an absentee ballot is important for voter confidence and something in which election administrators should invest their resources. It means that communication procedures – the forms in the absentee ballot materials or the instructions on the ballot itself – need to be improved.

Voter Identification

One last critical example is the case of voter identification. Numerous surveys have found that photo identification laws are often misapplied by poll workers. As Alvarez et al. (2009a) note, the SPAE found that "in the states that do not require photo ID in order to vote, one-quarter of all voters stated they were asked to show a photo ID at their polling place. In states that require all voters to show photo identification, roughly one-quarter of voters said they showed photo identification not because it was required but because it was convenient."[9] This failure to identify almost one-quarter of respondents correctly across most states illustrates a problem that, by using a performance metric, can be tracked across elections. The effectiveness of policy changes related to voter identification can also be tracked using such a metric.

A good example of how a metric can be used for both policy change and for performance measurement is the way in which data affected voter identification laws and practice in New Mexico. In 2006, New Mexico law required that voters identify themselves to the poll workers. The definition of identification was broadly defined and included a simple written or verbal statement attesting to a voter's name, year of birth, and the last four digits of the voter's Social Security number. Poll workers could only ask for physical identification from newly registered voters who were voting for the first time and who did not register with the county clerk.[10] The law gave poll workers discretion in how to implement the law, and the 2006 voter survey data showed that the New Mexico voter identification law was not implemented uniformly across precincts. Election Day, Hispanic, and male voters reported being more likely to show a physical form of identification, such as a voter registration card or a driver's license, than were early voters, non-Hispanics, and women (Atkeson et al. 2010e).

---

[9] http://vote.caltech.edu/drupal/files/report/2008%20Survey%20of%20the% 20Performance%20of%20American%20Elections%20Executive%20Summary .pdf, 2.

[10] This language is drawn from http://www.unm.edu/~atkeson/documents/NM_ Election_Report.pdf .

By comparison, that same year, a similar survey was conducted in Colorado's Seventh Congressional District, where the voter identification law required all voters to show some form of nonphoto or photo identification. There the law was applied almost uniformly across precincts; nearly all voters (95%) indicated that they provided some form of voter identification (Atkeson 2007a, 2007b). This comparison suggested that something was different about the New Mexico implementation of voter identification laws that warranted further investigation. This finding also shows how comparing across election jurisdictions can provide helpful feedback about the implementation of the process in one's own election jurisdiction.

In 2008, in the Election Day observations (a mode of evaluation we discuss later in Chapter 6), it was found that, once again, there was inconsistency in the implementation of voter identification laws. Although in some precincts, the poll workers followed the law and allowed voters to choose the identification process most comfortable to them, in many other cases, poll workers asked for a physical form of identification from voters. In some cases, we observed that workers changed this criterion across voters within the same precinct. Thus one voter might have been asked for photo identification, but another voter was only required to give her name. In 2010, we observed, and voter survey data again confirmed, that the implementation of the New Mexico voter identification laws was problematic. However, in 2010, we observed that the law was incorrectly applied more equally across different demographic groups of voters.

The metrics for studying voter identification in New Mexico also illustrate how surveys have to evolve so that the research question can be answered effectively. The voter identification law was first implemented in 2006, and in that year, the voter survey just included a simple question: "What type of identification did you have to show?" The survey response categories were as follows: (1) I did not have to show any identification, (2) registration card, (3) driver's license, (4) utility bill, and (5) other. Nearly two-thirds (65%) of these voters indicated that they provided some form of identification – answers 2–5 – and one-third (35%) indicated that they did not. Nearly two in four (41%) of those voters presented a driver's license, and 58 percent presented their voter registration cards; only 0.5 percent chose some other form of identification.

Given that we saw many voters choose the photo identification option in 2006, we needed to create a more precise metric to evaluate the photo identification implementation in New Mexico. To do this, the questions about how voter identification was implemented were broken down into several smaller parts. Specifically, the question was changed so that it better reflected state law. The law provides that

- the minimum identification required for each voter under state law is for her to state her name, address, and birth year.
- voters could also choose to show a physical form of identification, such as a voter registration card, driver's license, or utility bill. If the voter opted for a photographic identification, it did not have to contain the voter's address and if the voter opted for a non-photo form of identification, the document had to include an address, but it did not have to match the voter registration rolls (NMSA Section 1-1-24 1978).

In the telephone survey of voters, it was important first to determine which voters were asked for some sort of photo identification, so the question was asked, "When you went to vote, were you asked to show photo identification – like a driver's license?" Those who said no were asked, "How were you identified at the polls? Did you show your voter registration card or some other form of nonphoto identification?" Those who said no to this second question were asked, "Did you provide just your name, your name and address, your name and birth year, your name address and birth year, or something else?" Finally, those who gave a different response were then asked to explain how they were identified at the polls.

The results, presented in Table 3.2, show that voters report both that they were not asked for proper identification and were likely to be asked for information they did not need to provide. Specifically, 41 percent of voters were asked to show photo identification, one-quarter (25%) showed a registration card, another quarter provided verbal information that was incomplete, and about 1 in 10 (9%) verbally responded with the complete information required by law.

The other way we asked this question was in our mixed-mode Internet–mail survey. Because the survey was self-responding, we asked the following to obtain the precision that we needed: "When you went to vote, were you ASKED to show PHOTO-identification, like a

TABLE 3.2. *Frequency of Showing Different
Forms of Voter Identification*

Identification	Frequency
Driver's license	40.8
Voter registration card	25.2
Incorrect verbal ID	25.3
Correct verbal ID	8.7
TOTAL	100.0

Note: These data are from a telephone survey in New
Mexico. A different question was asked of Internet
voters. These data are shown in Table 4.3.

driver's license, did you just provide a PHOTO-ID to the poll worker
without them asking, or were you identified in some other way?"

Those who gave some other response were asked a follow-up question:

If you were not asked to show photo-identification or did not just automatically
provide ID to the poll worker, how were you identified at the polls? Did you:
(1) show your voter registration card, (2) state your name, (3) state your name
and address, (4) state your name and birth year, (5) I wrote my name, address
and birth year on a piece of paper, or (6) I did it another way."

Voters who did it another way were then asked to explain how they
were identified at the polls.

This question wording does two things. First, it is possible to determine if poll workers are asking for identification or if voters are offering
identification to the poll workers on their own. Second, because it is
possible to correct for voter actions with the first question, we can
be more confident in recoding the responses as voters being identified
correctly or incorrectly. Voters who provided an ID to poll workers
without being asked as well as those who correctly answered the verbal
or written statement were identified as correct. Those who indicated
they were asked to show photo identification or did not comply with
all the verbal requirements were counted as incorrect. The results once
again demonstrate that the law was applied correctly only half the time
for Election Day or early voters (51%). By asking the question in multiple parts, we can get a more accurate metric for voter identification.

This metric also allows us to determine if there are biases in implementation across races. Table 3.3 shows how this identification law

TABLE 3.3. *Frequency of Correct Voter Identification by Ethnicity, Internet Survey*

	Non-Hispanic	Hispanic
Correct	52.3	41.8
Incorrect	47.7	58.2
TOTAL	100.0	100.0

Note: These data are from an Internet survey in New Mexico. A different question was asked of telephone voters. These data are shown in Table 4.2.

was applied across Hispanic and non-Hispanic voters; there is evidence that Hispanics were more likely to be identified incorrectly. Specifically, a majority of self-identified non-Hispanics were identified correctly, but a majority of Hispanics were identified incorrectly. This finding is consistent with a recent national finding that showed that Hispanics were more likely to have to show stronger forms of identification than non-Hispanics (Alvarez et al. 2009a). In 2010, the law had not changed substantially, and we saw a similar result, except that there were no differences between whites and Hispanics in Election Day voting. Both were incorrectly identified at an equal rate (Atkeson et al. 2010c).

Of course, all voters should have to go through an identification process that complies with the law. The complexities of the New Mexico identification law, which has so many options for voters and hence so many options for poll workers, suggests that a better law would require the same form of identification – either verbal, written, or a stronger form of identification such as a physical form of identification or photo identification like a driver's license – of all voters and would not allow for so many choices (Atkeson et al. 2010c, 2010e; Alvarez et al. 2007a).

Applying Metrics to Management

For election administrators, the performance measurement data from voters are important for three reasons. First, the data allow them to see how their most important clients – voters – view the voting process. The experience that voters have is critical for evaluating the performance of the elections operation overall as well as the performance of specific precincts. We would note that other customers – political parties and candidates – can also be surveyed in a similar manner regarding issues that matter to them such as the campaign filing process or the process of getting election-related data (such as voter files and voting data).

Second, the metrics can be used to improve performance. Take the example of voter identification in New Mexico. The problem with voter identification is an important failure of performance by poll workers. Poll workers are implementing the law incorrectly and also doing so in a manner that seems to be discriminatory in nature. On the basis of these data, the election officials can attempt to address the problem through better training and materials and also through better signage that tells voters what to do to identify themselves at the polling location, and indeed, they have attempted to do so and continue to refine their training sessions with each subsequent election.

Third, the performance measurement data also provide the basis for the election officials to make a case to state election officials and to the legislature about the need to clarify the law. The data illustrate the problems that exist with the current law and provide the specificity needed so that policy makers can see how to change the law to address the problem most effectively. In this case, a legislative remedy is required, but other performance data might lead to new administrative rules or change in training on a local or statewide level.

Conclusions

The 2000 presidential election exposed a variety of weaknesses in the American electoral process – inferior voting equipment, poor poll worker training, bad ballot design, and problematic voter registries. But that election also demonstrated how little election officials and the research community knew about the experiences of voters when they attempted to vote, what problems they encountered with the registration process, why they did not vote, and how confident they were with the election process in general. Other than a few questions in the CPS Voting Supplement, and perhaps a stray question or two in other surveys, few data were collected prior to 2000 that attempted to assess in a systematic way the experiences of voters.

The situation began to change soon after, as researchers began to experiment with quantitative tools for assessing voter experiences (Bullock et al. 2005; Atkeson and Tafoya 2008; Alvarez and Hall 2004, 2008b). Then, in 2006 and 2008, more detailed state-level voter experience surveys began to be developed (e.g., in the New Mexico and Colorado projects), and efforts were made to collect detailed voter experience data across states (e.g., the 2008 Survey of the Performance of American Elections). These local, state, and national surveys have produced a wealth of data that have shown areas where election administration is successful and also places where administration needs to be improved.

For election administrators, having these data is critical because they provide systematic performance data that can be used to directly diagnose failures in the electoral process. The data at a state or county level, where administrative rules are more uniform, are particularly important for election officials. A survey of voters can provide the election officials with direct performance measurement data that cover the performance of numerous aspects of the electoral process that are generally unobservable or unknowable. For example, election officials cannot know about the absentee voting experience without asking because it occurs outside their purview. Likewise, whether voters understand aspects of the voting process, have difficulties with certain tasks, or have difficulty even finding the polling place cannot be known unless the voter is asked. These performance data provide election officials with an important tool for tuning the electoral machinery so that continuous improvements can be made to the process.

In this chapter, we have really only scratched the surface of how election officials can and should develop and implement voter experience studies. Entire textbooks have been written about both qualitative and quantitative methodologies for studying individual-level opinions and behavior; our intention in this chapter was not to provide an exhaustive text but instead to point to some important examples of recent efforts to study voting experiences. We believe that these examples demonstrate the utility of voter experience research, which is a rapidly evolving field of study for researchers and election officials alike.

Appendix: A Few Notes on Surveys and Focus Groups

In this chapter, we discuss both qualitative and quantitative means of studying voters and other key players in the election process. In this appendix, we delve into the nuanced issues associated with both focus groups and surveys.

Focus Groups

As we noted, focus groups are an effective way of getting qualitative information from a group of individuals. Here we discuss how focus groups can be designed and implemented in more detail.

We define a *focus group* as a fully moderated, structured, in-person, small-group research effort. We define each of those terms and provide an example from our recent research in Los Angeles County, where we conducted a comprehensive focus group study in spring 2010. Focus groups with these attributes are ideal for election performance evaluation.

First, in a fully moderated focus group, the discussion with group participants is led by an impartial and well-trained moderator. The role of the moderator is to lead the conversation with group participants through the complete study objectives (usually by following a discussion outline or guide) to ensure that all participants have the opportunity to have a say in the conversation and to subjectively move the conversation to either dig deeper into interesting points or to move along when it is clear that the conversation is lagging on a certain point.

Second, a well-conducted focus group needs to be structured. That structure begins with the research team articulating the general goals of the focus group study, and then, from those goals, developing a series of research questions or specific hypotheses that will be tested in the focus groups. These questions or hypotheses then form the foundation from which the research team develops the focus group guidelines – a written outline or document that translates the research questions into a series of questions that the moderator can use to lead the discussion.

Third, a focus group needs to be a face-to-face conversation. This is one of the most important aspects of a focus group: that it is a face-to-face and dynamic conversation among a small group of individuals. The face-to-face nature of a focus group is efficient and cost effective and allows participants to consider arguments and the opinions of other participants. It is thus a good opportunity to study opinions about issues that participants may not have thought much about in the past and to see how their opinions and responses can be affected by different arguments and new points of view. However, the face-to-face environment is also potentially problematic; without good group moderation, conversations can be taken over by particularly aggressive or opinionated participants, and the conversation can go in unproductive directions.

Fourth, a focus group is a small-group effort. Typically, a focus group involves 8 to 12 participants. Fewer than 8 participants is oftentimes too small a group to develop a conversation; with more than a dozen, it is often difficult to have a forum in which all participants can provide input, and a large group creates incentives for some participants to free ride and be less involved. Recruitment of participants will depend on the objectives of the research questions at hand; typically, it is most helpful to recruit participants from only certain demographic groups (e.g., by age cohort), but in other cases, it might be productive for a focus group project to have a more broadly representative set of participants, and such decisions may influence the feedback received. However, it is imperative that any focus group effort involve a limited number of participants to ensure that all participants have an opportunity to express their opinions and to engage fully in the group's conversation.

A discussion guide for a focus group is necessary so that the moderator knows what questions to ask and how to frame the discussion so that he can keep the discussion focused and on track. The discussion guides developed for the VSAP focus groups started off with a detailed introduction, with the moderator discussing the purposes of the focus group. The moderator then discussed the ground rules, emphasizing

- that there are no right or wrong answers
- that everyone needs to say his piece but not engage in long speeches
- that responses were being recorded and transcribed but that the participants' identities would be kept anonymous in any reports
- that there were people behind the one-way mirror who were listening to the focus group

The goal of the focus groups in Los Angles was to ensure that each group had a similar experience in that each discussed the same topics and touched on the same key points. The structured nature of the focus group and the discussion guide helped to ensure that this would occur. Once the focus groups were completed, transcripts were produced and analyzed.

Designing Voter Experience Surveys

When local election officials or researchers conduct surveys – especially for the purpose of promoting performance measurement – the most important question that has to be answered is also the most simple: what question (or questions) or performance measures is the survey intended to answer? By carefully delineating these questions, the survey can be effectively designed to ensure that all performance data based on voter attitudes and experiences can be captured during the survey process. There is a good database of such questions that election officials can use, including questions from the SPAE, the VSAP, and the New Mexico study, as well as from the American National Election Study. By using previously tested questions, election officials can know that the questions work well at addressing the metric of interest.

Before initiation of a survey research project, those involved need to determine what research questions are part of the survey effort, what resources can be brought to the survey project, and what degree of survey accuracy is needed to answer the research questions. This type of calculation is widely used in the survey research world, having been popularized by Robert Groves.[11] The idea here is to always keep in mind that because surveys are not censuses, there will always be error in the survey results. Typically, a survey will rely on some type of sample, and because the sample does not include all the voters in the jurisdiction's population, there will always be sampling error. When you hear that a survey is accurate with a margin of error of plus or minus 3 percent, this is the sampling error.

It is also important to remember that the overall survey sampling error for a survey is only true for the total number of cases, not any subsample. For example, if the overall survey has 900 respondents, the margin of error is likely to be plus or minus 3 percent. However, if 200 of the respondents are African American and 200 are Latino, then the margin of error for each subsample is going to be larger than 3 percent (actually, it will be almost 6%). So if an election official is interested in the attitudes of African American or Latino voters in a predominately white jurisdiction, efforts may have to be taken to

---

[11] Groves (2004) presents these ideas in his book *Survey Errors and Survey Costs*.

survey more members of these groups than would occur if voters were surveyed using solely a random contacting methodology.

Surveys have other sources of error as well, arising from how much time and effort can be put into contacting and interviewing everyone selected for a sample, making sure that the questions are asked in ways that are generally error-free, and so on.

There are two important considerations to keep in mind, however, about the trade-offs associated with resources and survey error. First, regardless of available resources, there will always be survey error. Resources can minimize survey error, but the nature of survey research is that it will always produce estimates of voter opinions and experiences. Those estimates will have some degree of error associated with them. Second, a lack of substantial resources should not drive a research team to give up on efforts to implement voter experience surveys; rather, a lack of resources simply will lead the research team to rely on methodologies that will likely produce more survey error.

To return to the VSAP example, the research team was focused on trying to minimize a variety of survey errors. First, Los Angeles County has a very large population of registered voters: nearly 4.4 million as of spring 2010. Given the large population of registered voters, the research team knew that they needed relatively large samples of registered voters, more than 1,000 in total. Second, the research team was concerned about the possibility that different methods of survey sampling and interviewing might affect the patterns of responses measured by the survey project, so the research team decided to utilize a mixed-mode survey design, with 500 registered voters interviewed in a nonprobability sample online and over 500 registered voters in a probability-based sampling interviewed by telephone.

A mixed-mode design is one that allows respondents to be contacted or respond to surveys across multiple formats (Dillman 2000). Mixed-mode surveys are becoming the normal way of doing surveys because of the number of individuals who do not have landline telephones and because of the costs associated with doing telephone surveys as opposed to Internet surveys. The New Mexico survey also used a mixed-mode design.

Third, the research team was also concerned about possible errors that might arise if the interviews did not explicitly allow registered

voters to provide their answers in their language of choice, so the
research team wished to allow some respondents to answer the survey
in either Spanish or Mandarin Chinese. Fourth, the research team was
concerned that the telephone interviewing methodology (which was
based on a sample drawn from the list of registered voters in the
county, augmented by a private firm with telephone numbers) needed
to allow for some of the interviewing to be done on mobile or cellular
telephones.[12]

Finally, the research team was concerned about error arising from
questionnaire design. So the research team did something that is quite
common in the survey research field – as much as they could, they
used survey questions that had been included in previous surveys, in
which they had a high degree of confidence. For example, most of the
questions used in the VSAP survey had been used in a similar national
voter experience survey that the VSAP research team had conducted in
2008 and from other election administration surveys with which VSAP
were familiar (Alvarez et al. 2009a; Atkeson 2007a, 2007b). The point
here is that an examination of academic surveys could suggest a lot
of strong questions to ask to examine election administration in any
state or area, and we include a sample of these potential questions in
the appendix in the back of the book. We think these questions offer
valuable information and are ready for use. It is also important to test
your survey ahead of time. This can be easily done by using election
staff, family, and friends to pretest the survey and provide feedback
on its length and understandability. Pretesting is a critical aspect of
good survey design, and we strongly suggest that researchers test their
questionnaires before implementation.

These considerations led to the following mixed-mode implementation for the VSAP surveys: a total of 651 interviews were completed
by telephone, with 80 cell phone respondents, 25 Mandarin Chinese
respondents, and 51 Spanish respondents. Five hundred interviews
were done online, with all of the interviewing completed by the end

---

[12] Surveying individuals on their cell phones is becoming more and more important.
According to the Centers for Disease Control and Prevention, "more than one of
every five American homes (20.2%) had only wireless telephones (also known as
cellular telephones, cell phones, or mobile phones) during the second half of 2008,
an increase of 2.7 percentage points since the first half of 2008." http://www.cdc.
gov/nchs/data/nhis/earlyrelease/wireless200905.htm.

of March 2010. The results of the VSAP surveys found that, overall, most Los Angeles County voters, without information to the contrary, did not think that the existing InkaVote system should be replaced. Only 21 percent of the telephone sample and 14 percent of the Internet sample said it should be replaced. But the survey also found that these opinions might be malleable; registered voters in the sample were also asked which kind of voting system they would most prefer to vote on. In both samples, a plurality of respondents said that they would prefer to vote on an electronic voting machine (43% in the telephone sample and 28% in the Internet sample).

The New Mexico study provides a nice example of how to select voters in the sample. First, for studying elections, it is generally the case that the proper sampling frame – the population being sampled – is the jurisdiction's voter registration file. This approach is easy to use for finding voters, and it is much cheaper than a random-digit dialing approach, which would lead to many calls not only to nonvoters but also to many unregistered voters. Second, using the voter file also allows for what is referred to as vote validation. Vote validation is important for ensuring that people who answered the survey actually voted. People often lie about their voting experiences, and vote validation allows surveyors to ensure that the survey respondents actually did vote. Vote validation provides the necessary information to determine the actual sample size since a number of sample members did not participate in the election. Third, the voter registration file provided additional accurate information about the demographic characteristics of the sample, allowing us to examine the representativeness of the sample respondents (see Atkeson et al. 2011b).

When conducting a survey, there are also basic steps for ensuring that the survey has a good response rate. Here we consider how this was done in the New Mexico case. First, those to be surveyed were sent a letter by mail requesting their participation in our Election Administration Survey. The letter explained our study and provided a Web address that took respondents to a Web page through which they could respond to the survey. The letter also explained that respondents could request a mail survey by contacting us via a toll-free number. Sample registered voters who did not respond were sent up to three reminder postcards. The research team constructed this mixed-mode survey to control costs, while trying to maintain good coverage, recognizing that many voters likely did not have access to the Internet and therefore needed an alternative response mode.

Nonprobability Sampling and Other Ways to Interview Voters

Readers are no doubt familiar with other types of surveys, for example, exit polls and research projects whereby survey respondents are not selected by probability sampling. We have presented a mix of these types of studies in this section. The VSAP study, for example, had a nonprobability sample component, the Internet study, and a list-based probability phone survey. Because probability-based studies have the strongest scientific foundations, they are likely the most desirable, but even nonprobability studies, we argue, can be useful. A probability sample is one in which someone can compute the probability that a specific individual in the population might be selected for inclusion in the survey; this property allows researchers to use standard tools of statistical inference to estimate quantities of interest from the survey data.

Surveys in which voters are not selected for inclusion into the survey using some method that ensures that the probabilities of selection are known are called *nonprobability samples*.[13] Good examples are exit polls; there voters from selected precincts are interviewed, but because one does not select the participants at random in advance of the survey (in fact, in advance of a survey, little is known about the nature of the potential respondents), we cannot estimate the probabilities of inclusion, nor can we necessarily use standard tools of statistical inference.

Though this does mean that, if possible, researchers should use probability sampling methods, we also are cognizant of the fact that sometimes resources are so limited that nonprobability methods need to be used. Though nonprobability designs can be used if resources are limited, they should be used with care and only when necessary. If it is possible to use probability sampling methods, then researchers should employ such techniques for voter experience surveys.

It is also possible for researchers to use combined, or mixed-mode, survey designs. An example might be a situation in which the researcher

---

[13] An excellent introduction to nonprobability and self-completion surveys is Dillman et al. (2009).

wished to combine the scientific power associated with a probability design with the cost effectiveness of a nonprobability sample. In such an application, the research team could use a randomly selected telephone survey sample in addition to an exit poll of voters leaving precincts on Election Day. Mixed-mode designs are increasingly popular designs, but they can produce complexities that need careful consideration (Dillman et al. 2009; Atkeson and Tafoya 2008; Atkeson et al. 2011b).

4

Measuring the Performance of Poll Workers

For a majority of voters in a majority of states, the voting experience involves going to a polling place – either in early voting or on Election Day – and casting a ballot. In that visit to the polling place, it is with the poll workers whom the voter interacts. As several authors have noted (e.g., Hall et al. 2007, 2008, 2009), poll workers are what are typically referred to as *street-level bureaucrats*. The term *bureaucrat* is not meant here as a pejorative; rather, it reflects that fact that, in a polling place, the poll worker makes an array of decisions that determine the experience that each and every voter has. Perhaps the most important decision a poll workers makes is whether a person is an eligible voter and whether she will get a regular ballot, a provisional ballot, or no ballot at all. Poll workers also determine whether to ask a voter to show identification – a decision that may or may not follow the state's law (Atkeson et al. 2010e). The ability of a poll worker to follow the directions and complete a provisional ballot form correctly may determine whether a voter's ballot gets counted. This is just part of a larger list of ways in which poll workers make decisions that directly affect the experience that voters have at the polling place and the general functioning and operations of the precinct.

For the local election officials (LEOs) across the country, monitoring these polling places to ensure that poll workers are conducting their business appropriately can be a difficult task. In any election jurisdictions with more than a handful of polling places, the LEOs are forced essentially to delegate the effective operation of the polls to their poll workers. This delegation creates what we typically refer to as a principal-agent problem (Alvarez and Hall 2006). Principal-agent problems are common throughout life. Say you need the plumbing fixed in your house. You could do it yourself, but you may not have the time or the skill to do it. Instead, you (the principal) decide to hire a plumber (an agent) to do the work for you. Now the problems arise. First, how do you know you picked the right plumber? Perhaps you received a recommendation from a friend or looked the person up on a website that rates plumbers. The problem with picking a plumber is that the plumber has every incentive to oversell his plumbing skills to you and to understate the actual cost of the job. In short, it is easy to pick the wrong plumber. Second, once you pick a plumber, it is hard to know if the plumber is doing what you need to have done. If the plumber tells you that you have to replace something, you probably do not have the skills to question his recommendation. Moreover, it can be hard to know if the plumber is working hard or shirking (slacking off). In short, monitoring the work is difficult.

Election officials face the same challenges in their job when it comes to running an election. They need to staff polling places, yet identifying the people who can do this – the poll workers – can be a difficult task. Poll workers have to be recruited and trained, and then the election officials have to hope that they will arrive at the requisite time – often 6:00 A.M. on Election Day – for their first and only day on the job. Although election officials can screen poll worker job candidates, there often are not large numbers of surplus poll workers among whom to discriminate.

Even if the election officials are able to pick quality poll workers, they still have the monitoring problem on Election Day. The poll workers may pass the hiring screens and be trained but still do things in the polls on Election Day that are problematic such as wrongly implementing the state law for authenticating voters or not providing a voter not on the voter rolls with a provisional ballot. Given the number of polling locations that may exist in a jurisdiction and their geographic distribution, it is likely to be very difficult for the election officials to monitor and take corrective action in every polling place and identify problems that arise related to the work of the poll workers.

For election officials and poll workers alike, every election can seem like a new event. Jurisdiction-wide elections are typically held infrequently – perhaps one or two elections per year – and state legislators may have made legal changes in the interim that make the process of running some aspect of the election new and unique. For example, in 2004 and 2006 in New Mexico, the elections were fundamentally different compared to the general election of 2008. In 2004 in New Mexico, most voters and poll workers cast ballots on electronic voting machines; in 2006, all voters were voting on paper ballots that were then scanned by an optical scan tabulator. In 2008, the laws related to voter identification had changed, and there was a large percentage increase in the number of voters who were casting votes during early voting. These changes can greatly affect the dynamic of the voting process for voters in the field and require election officials to change the way they train poll workers about the election process.

Measuring the Performance of Poll Workers

The measurement of the performance of poll workers can occur in two ways. First, it is possible to survey poll workers in the same way as voters are surveyed. Poll worker surveys have the same issues of sampling as well; it is important that poll worker surveys have as broad of coverage as possible. One way that this can be accomplished is by surveying at least one poll worker in every precinct. For instance, in 2008 in New Mexico, we developed a sampling procedure that had two components. First, because the poll workers in each precinct are part of a precinct board, headed by a presiding judge, we included the presiding judge from every precinct in the counties we examined in our sample. The precinct presiding judges receive additional training more carefully covering procedures for opening, closing, ballot reconciliation, provisional balloting, and other procedures and are responsible for the conduct of the election in their precinct and the various management activities at the polls. Presiding judges are the poll workers most likely to engage the voter and the precinct system at all possible points.[1] Second, we also randomly selected two additional members

---

[1] In New Mexico, technically, there are three poll worker positions: the presiding judge, the election judge, and the clerk. However, in terms of practice, there is the presiding

of the precinct board – poll clerks – from every precinct in each county to include in the sample. In Bernalillo County, we also selected an additional two sample members from each precinct because they had put together a larger precinct board than the other counties in our study.

Once we had completed the sampling process, we then surveyed the poll workers using a standard set of poll worker survey questions that have been used in numerous jurisdictions in the United States, including Ohio, Utah, California, New Mexico, Iowa, and Washington, D.C.[2] These surveys cover five types of questions:

- What motivated the poll worker to take the job and how was he recruited?
- How would he evaluate his training?
- How would he evaluate his experience on Election Day?
- How would he evaluate the quality of the election procedures?
- What are his personal demographic characteristics?

Having these data are important for the election official because they provide key information needed for managing the organization. With these data, the election official not only can measure performance but also has critical information related to the motivation of his employees, the skill sets that they bring to the various tasks involved in the election process, and the interaction of the worker with the various technologies employed in elections. This information provides the basic building blocks for election management (Rainey and Steinbauer 1999).

Demographics

Perhaps the most important thing from which election officials can benefit is understanding the demographics of their workers. Although the media often refer to poll workers as all being 72 years old, the data from poll worker surveys show that the average age of poll workers can vary widely across local jurisdictions. As we see in Table 4.1, in New

judge, who is the authority in the precinct and receives additional training to perform his job, and everyone else.
[2] Brigham Young University's Center for the Study of Elections and Democracy has a catalog of such questions.

TABLE 4.1. *Demographics of Poll Workers by County (in %)*

		Bernalillo	San Juan	Doña Ana	Santa Fe	Total
Age and gender	Average age	58.8	56.2	60.1	58.5	58.3
	Percentage male	32.2	17.1	33.7	21.8	30.7
Race	White	56.5	62.4	65.8	46.0	57.0
	African American	3.1	1.5	1.8	0.5	2.5
	Native American	2.7	28.5	0.6	4.5	4.4
	Hispanic	33.4	6.7	29.1	46.0	32.2
Education	High school or less	19.4	26.1	15.3	31	20.3
	Some college	35.3	55.7	37.1	37.4	37.3
	College degree or more	45.3	18.2	47.6	31.6	42.4
Employment status	Full time	22.2	20.3	20.3	15.4	21.5
	Part time	12.4	13.4	7.4	14.0	11.9
	Unemployed	6.0	7.2	5.5	6.2	5.8
	Student	4.4	1.0	5.6	2.1	4.8
	Retired	48.7	38.4	51.4	54.3	48.2
	Homemaker	6.3	19.7	9.8	8.0	7.8
Comfort with computers	Very comfortable	50.5	36.6	54.0	48.7	50.6
	Somewhat comfortable	30.2	35.0	28.4	30.7	29.8
	Not very comfortable	10.7	13.9	8.2	9.4	10.5
	Not at all comfortable	8.6	14.5	9.4	11.2	9.1
Frequency of Internet use	Once or more a day	55.2	35.9	60.3	50.5	54.3
	A few times a week	16.3	21.1	11.5	13.5	15.9
	A few times a month	5.0	6.9	5.0	5.6	5.3
	Hardly ever	9.3	17.2	6.9	10.3	9.6
	Never	14.2	18.9	16.3	20.1	14.9
Party identification	Democrat	61.5	42.4	49.2	68.6	59.1
	Independent	5.4	0.6	5.3	6.6	5.4
	Republican	30.8	54.3	42.8	21.8	33.1
Ideological attitudes	Very liberal	14.8	7.1	5.6	14.7	13.2
	Somewhat liberal	22.2	9.6	19.5	26.7	21.8
	Moderate	29.1	25.1	20.7	33.8	28.5
	Somewhat conservative	18.2	22.4	25.8	14.2	18.5
	Very conservative	11.4	23.9	21.7	7.8	13.2

TABLE 4.2. *Evaluation of Fellow Poll Workers and Previous Work Activity*

		Total
Likelihood of being a poll worker again	Very likely	80.1
	Somewhat likely	15.1
How would you rate the overall performance	1 to 7	13.8
of your fellow poll workers? (1 = very poor;	8	20.3
10 = excellent)	9	24.2
	10	41.7
How would you rate the overall performance	1 to 7	19.1
of your presiding judge? (1 = very poor;	8	10.8
10 = excellent, clerks only)	9	17.3
	10	52.8
Did you ever feel intimidated by the poll	Yes	11.4
watchers and/or poll challengers?	No	88.6
First election worked	Before 1990	14.9
	1991–2000	20.3
	2001–2008	64.8
Number of elections worked	0	4.5
	1	29.7
	2 to 5	34.0
	6 to 10	19.1
	More than 10	12.7

Mexico, most poll workers are female (69%) and are roughly 58 years old. We can also compare the county's poll worker populations to Census data and see that San Juan County's percentage of Native American poll workers (29%) is representative of its Native American population characteristics and that there are fewer Hispanic poll workers in San Juan and Doña Ana counties compared to their Census-estimated Hispanic populations. There are also differences across New Mexican counties regarding the educational attainment of poll workers and their level of computer experience and Internet savvy.

Demographic data can also allow the election officials to see the level of balance they have between political parties among their poll workers. For example, in Table 4.1, we see that Bernalillo and Santa Fe counties tend to have a higher proportion of Democratic poll workers, but San Juan and Doña Ana counties have somewhat more balance between the two parties. We can also compare data from the voter registration file to the poll worker surveys. Doing this, we see that Santa Fe County is 63 percent Democratic among its voters and that

San Juan County is 46 percent Republican.[3] Ideologically, most poll workers in our survey are also middle of the road, either identifying as moderates or somewhat liberal or somewhat conservative.

The survey data also allow election officials to determine the most effective means of recruiting poll workers. In general, most people seek out the job or are recruited by another poll worker. However, in Doña Ana County, political party officials also recruit many poll workers, and in Bernalillo County, many poll workers are recruited through advertising. The survey data also show that, when asked why they were poll workers, the three statements most poll workers strongly agreed with were (1) "it is my duty as a citizen," (2) "I am the kind of person who does my share," and (3) "I wanted to learn about the election process."

It is also possible to use the surveys to gather information about the performance of other poll workers and the experience that the workers had. In Table 4.2, we see that 95 percent of poll workers said they are either very likely (80%) or somewhat likely (15%) to be a poll worker again.[4] We also see that two-thirds of poll workers rate the overall performance of their colleagues as a 9 (24%) or a 10 (42%) on a 1–10 scale (where 10 is excellent); only 14 percent rate a 7 or lower. Because this question had been asked on a poll worker survey in 2006, it is possible to compare the two elections. When this is done, it shows that poll workers rated their colleagues substantially higher in 2008 compared to 2006, when one-quarter of poll workers rated their colleagues 7 or lower and just over one-quarter (27%) rated their colleagues a 10. The poll workers were also asked to rate the presiding judge – the chief poll worker – in their precinct. Over half (53%) of poll workers who were not presiding judges rated their presiding judge excellent (a 10 on a 1–10 scale); only 14 percent rated their judge a 5 or lower, and less than a quarter (19%) rated the presiding judge a 7 or lower.

---

[3] These data come from the voter registration report for the 2008 general election created by the secretary of state and available at http://www.sos.state.nm.us/sos-elections.html.

[4] We do not divide the data by county unless doing so is of substantive interest. County frequencies are detailed in the frequency report located in the appendix to Chapter 3.

When asked about poll watchers and challengers, 11 percent of poll workers stated that at one point or another, they felt intimidated by poll watchers or challengers. In Santa Fe, that rate was nearly twice as high, at over one in five (21%). Also, contrary to popular opinion, most poll workers have not been working as poll workers for a long time. In fact, 65 percent started after the 2000 election. Between 13 percent (Bernalillo County) and 22 percent (San Juan County) have been working at the job for more than 20 years, but most poll workers have worked in fewer than six elections.

Training

Poll worker surveys are also helpful in evaluating training. Several studies have found that the quality of the training poll workers receive affects their job satisfaction and their confidence that the ballots cast will be counted correctly (Hall et al. 2008). In 2008, almost all New Mexico poll workers stated that they attended at least one training session, and most of the poll workers who did not attend a training session were poll workers in previous elections. Importantly, presiding judges who are responsible for the management of the precinct were more likely to have had more training and to have worked more elections than precinct clerks. Only in Doña Ana County did more than 5 percent of poll workers report not attending at least one training session. Most poll workers attend one training session, but nearly 3 in 10 (30%) poll workers attended two or more training sessions.[5] Between 89 percent and 96 percent of poll workers received a manual, booklet, or DVD at their training, and about 6 in 10 (62%) poll workers said that they actually read all of the materials before Election Day. Again, comparing 2006 survey data with 2008 survey data, it is possible to determine that more poll workers received take-home training materials in 2008. A majority of poll workers who received a DVD or video watched it before the election, which is roughly equivalent to what we saw in 2006. These data suggest that over the two elections, there were

[5] Some research has found little relationship between having poll workers attend more than one training session and their performance on Election Day, assuming the one session is effective. See Hall et al. (2008).

TABLE 4.3. *Poll Worker Evaluation of Training*

| | Percent Answering Strongly Agree | | | | |
	Bernalillo	San Juan	Doña Ana	Santa Fe	Total
After the training, I was confident in my ability to do my job on Election Day	52.5	72.9	54.3	64.6	54.8
The training was easy to understand	57.5	75.5	57.4	60.5	59.0
The training was hands-on, not just a lecture	38.3	48.2	29.8	39.8	38.4
The training sessions spent enough time covering election law and procedures	47.1	65.8	43.5	56.0	49.1
The training sessions were boring or too long	7.1	8.2	13.1	6.9	7.9
I would have liked more training	14.6	16.2	16.1	13.3	14.3
The training prepared me well for Election Day	36.7	57.8	45.4	48.1	40.5
The training prepared me well for handling provisional ballots	36.7	57.8	45.4	48.1	40.5
The training prepared me well for handling spoiled ballots	38.6	60.3	47.6	51.8	42.5

some improvement in efforts to reach more poll workers with training materials.

The critical question with training is whether the poll workers felt that their training left them feeling confident in their ability to do their work on Election Day. Table 4.3 shows that just over half of poll workers in Bernalillo and Doña Ana counties, 65 percent in Santa Fe County, and 73 percent in San Juan County strongly agreed that they were confident in their ability to do their job. San Juan County poll workers were also the most likely to strongly agree that the training was easy to understand and that they were trained well to handle provisional ballots and spoiled ballots. Also, 73 percent of poll workers in San Juan County – compared to just under half of those in Bernalillo and Doña Ana counties – stated that they strongly agreed that they were well prepared for Election Day.

The survey data showed some important differences between San Juan County and the other three counties in the training related to spoiled and provisional ballots. Given that a voter who either casts a provisional ballot or has a spoiled ballot is likely to be troubled by the experience, encountering a less than well-trained poll worker could exacerbate the voter's concerns about this process.

The data suggest three factors that may explain why the San Juan County poll workers feel more confident and prepared. First, San Juan County poll workers were much more likely than the poll workers in the other counties to strongly agree that training was hands-on, not just a lecture. Other studies have found that poll workers in counties with more hands-on training also feel more confident in their ability to do their job (Hall et al. 2009). In addition, the poll workers in San Juan County were also much more likely than the poll workers in other counties to strongly agree that the training sessions spent enough time covering election law and procedures. San Juan County also had the highest number of experienced poll workers, which may have contributed to these differences as well.

Evaluating Procedures

On Election Day, poll workers have a set of written instructions and procedures they must follow. Poll worker surveys are a means of evaluating the clarity and effectiveness of these procedures. In Table 4.4, we see that 74 percent of poll workers across the four counties thought that the instructions for opening the polls were very clear, and just over two-thirds of poll workers thought that the procedures for closing the polls were clear. Three-fourths of poll workers thought that the instructions for securing the ballots during and after the election were clear. The weakest area, where the instructions were thought to be least clear, was with regard to the clarity of the procedures for reconciling the number of ballots cast and the number of voters who

TABLE 4.4. *Election Day Procedures by County*

		Bernalillo	San Juan	Doña Ana	Santa Fe	Total
The instructions for opening the polls	Very clear	71.2	78.8	80.7	84.2	73.9
When to ask a voter for her identification before voting	Very clear	70.4	82.6	74.3	76.8	72.1
The instructions for closing the polls at the end of the day	Very clear	62.8	78.2	71.1	79.6	65.9
The printed instruction materials we used when we had a procedural question	Very clear	53.0	75.4	49.7	62.7	55.2
The instructions for reconciling the number of voters voting and the number of ballots cast	Very clear	56.4	73.4	54.1	71.9	58.5
Securing the ballots during and after the election	Very clear	72.6	86.0	77.7	86.1	75.1
How different was your training from your experience on Election Day?	Very different	5.3	4.8	3.3	1.5	4.9
	Somewhat different	25.9	21.4	21.2	21.5	25.1
	Not too different	42.9	37.1	49.2	41.7	42.9
	Not at all different	23.9	34.3	22.2	34.8	24.9
	I didn't attend training	2.0	2.4	4.1	0.5	2.2

voted. A majority of poll workers – almost 60 percent – said that those instructions were clear, but it was rated lowest of all of the areas examined. For the local election officials, this finding suggests that additional training is needed regarding how to perform vote reconciliation. Finally, 55 percent of poll workers thought that the printed instruction materials used to answer procedural questions were very clear.

Collecting similar poll worker data over time allows us to compare the attitudes of poll workers regarding the quality of the training and instructions across elections. When we do that here, we see that attitudes were, in general, largely similar across elections. However, in Doña Ana County, poll workers perceived major improvement in the quality of the poll opening instructions (69% in 2006 compared to 81% in 2008) and poll closing instructions (64% in 2006 compared to 71% in 2008). Santa Fe County also received higher marks for the quality of the instructions for securing the ballots in 2008 (81% in 2006 compared to 86% in 2008). However, all three counties examined in 2006 showed a decline in the evaluation of the instructions for reconciling the ballots at the end of the day. The evaluation on this metric in Bernalillo County declined from 71 percent in 2006 to 56 percent in 2008. In Doña Ana County, it declined from 74 percent to 54 percent, and in Santa Fe County, it declined from 78 percent to 72 percent. Further analysis determined that instructions provided by the secretary of state's office were incorrect and were in conflict with instructions provided by the county clerks. These differences likely caused confusion for the poll workers and resulted in a more difficult reconciliation process.

One clear way of evaluating the quality of training is to know if the poll workers perceived their Election Day experiences as being different from the training that they received. Relatively few poll workers thought that their election experiences were very different from their training, but between 23 percent (in San Juan, Doña Ana, and Santa Fe counties) and 30 percent (in Bernalillo County) thought that their training was very or somewhat different from their Election Day experience. When we compare these attitudes over time, we see that poll workers in 2008 were much less likely to say that their training was different from Election Day compared to 2006. Although the question wording was slightly different, we found that fully one-quarter of poll workers thought that the training and the Election Day experience in 2006 were "a lot" different, compared to a mere 1 in 20 in 2008 who thought they were "very different."[6]

---

[6] In 2006, we asked this as a two-part question, first asking if it was different and then how it was different. By removing the "not at all different" category from the 2008 numbers and recalculating the percentages, we create roughly comparable measures.

Problems at the Polls

Poll worker survey data can also identify problems that occurred on Election Day, from missing poll workers to problems with voting equipment. In the survey from 2008, it was possible to determine that between 78 percent and 90 percent of poll workers said that all of their poll workers showed up on time. We could also determine that between 23 percent and 36 percent of poll workers said there were conflicts between poll workers on Election Day. We also see that a small but significant number of poll workers said that there were problems with voting equipment, ballots, and the procedures associated with handling ballots. Just over 20 percent of poll workers said that they had a problem with their AutoMARK voting device over the course of the day. Similar percentages of poll workers noted problems with their optical scan ballot reader over the course of their day.

The survey data also provide important metrics regarding the need to contact the county election office and the responsiveness of the office. About three in four poll workers said that they called the county election office during the day, although 92 percent of San Juan County poll workers said that they contacted the office during the day. However, only 43 percent of Doña Ana County poll workers thought their county election office was easy to contact, compared to 61 percent in Bernalillo County, 89 percent in San Juan County, and 85 percent in Santa Fe County. But once they got through, about 85 percent of all poll workers thought that the county clerks were very responsive.

In Table 4.5, we show how the poll workers evaluated activities on Election Day. First, 90 percent of poll workers said that there were no problems setting up the optical scanners, and similar percentages said there were no problems shutting down the optical scanners. Likewise, most poll workers said that the AutoMARK was easy to set up. However, the fact that 10 percent of poll workers found the equipment somewhat or very problematic to set up or shut down is significant. There is only one scanner per precinct, and a problem setting it up or closing it down could affect the election process, and potentially the result, in a high-profile election. Second, most poll workers either strongly agreed (25%) or somewhat strongly agreed (55%) that the AutoMARK worked well, but fewer than 4 in 10 (36%) encouraged voters who made mistakes and spoiled their ballots to use the machine

TABLE 4.5. *Poll Worker Evaluations of Election Day (in %)*

		Total
There were problems setting up the optical ballot scanner in my voting location	Somewhat disagree	50.3
	Strongly disagree	39.9
There were problems shutting down the optical ballot scanner at the end of the day and reporting the results	Somewhat disagree	50.0
	Strongly disagree	42.6
There were many provisional ballots resulting from voter identification challenges	Somewhat disagree	53.1
	Strongly disagree	31.2
There were problems setting up the AutoMARK in my voting location	Somewhat disagree	49.5
	Strongly disagree	39.8
Voters who used the AutoMARK thought it worked well	Strongly agree	24.8
	Somewhat agree	54.9
	Somewhat disagree	10.5
	Strongly disagree	9.8
We encouraged voters who spoiled a ballot to vote using the AutoMARK	Strongly agree	9.1
	Somewhat agree	27.0
	Somewhat disagree	42.6
	Strongly disagree	21.3
Generally speaking, voters were satisfied with the paper ballots and optical scan voting process	Strongly agree	46.0
	Somewhat agree	46.2
	Somewhat disagree	4.6
	Strongly disagree	3.2

to cast their second ballots. Third, 92 percent of the poll workers thought that voters were very satisfied or somewhat satisfied with the optical scan voting system. However, San Juan County poll workers felt significantly different from the other counties' poll workers on this matter; only about four in five (79%) indicated that they strongly or somewhat agreed that voters were satisfied with the optical scan voting system.

Confidence and Satisfaction

One bottom-line metric for evaluating the performance-based management is to consider poll worker satisfaction with their performance and their confidence that the votes in the election were counted accurately. Table 4.6 shows that in 2008, almost all poll workers were very satisfied or somewhat satisfied with their performance as a poll

TABLE 4.6. *Poll Worker Satisfaction in Percentages by County*

		Bernalillo	San Juan	Doña Ana	Santa Fe	Total
Satisfaction with	Very satisfied	85.0	88.0	81.2	90.6	85.1
performance as	Somewhat satisfied	13.7	11.1	18.0	9.4	13.9
poll worker	Somewhat dissatisfied	0.8	0.9	0.0	0.0	0.6
	Very dissatisfied	0.5	0.0	0.8	0.0	0.4
Confidence that	Very confident	86.9	90.1	81.7	93.6	86.4
votes counted	Somewhat confident	10.4	8.3	13.6	6.2	10.7
accurately in						
their voting	Not very confident	0.9	0.0	2.2	0.0	1.0
location	Not at all confident	0.3	0.0	0.6	0.0	0.3
	Don't know	1.5	1.6	1.9	0.2	1.6
Confidence that	Very confident	41.1	71.2	28.2	56.5	43.0
votes counted	Somewhat confident	36.0	18.2	39.9	22.0	34.5
accurately in						
other voting	Not very confident	2.9	0.0	3.7	0.6	2.7
locations in	Not at all confident	0.7	0.6	1.6	0.6	0.7
county	Don't know	19.3	10.0	26.6	20.3	19.1
Confidence that	Very confident	23.4	25.7	16.3	28.3	23.5
votes counted	Somewhat confident	41.9	34.7	34.5	32.9	40.0
accurately						
in other	Not very confident	5.9	10.8	9.1	8.6	6.8
counties in	Not at all confident	1.7	4.4	3.2	1.6	2.0
New Mexico	Don't know	27.1	24.4	36.9	28.6	27.7

worker. These performance ratings are significantly higher than the poll worker evaluations from 2006. In 2006, not quite two-thirds (64%) of Bernalillo County poll workers were "very satisfied," 6 in 10 (57%) in Doña Ana County were "very satisfied," and three-quarters (78%) in Santa Fe County were "very satisfied." The increase by over 20 percentage points for both Doña Ana and Bernalillo counties, and a 12 percentage point increase in Santa Fe County, is a strong indicator of performance improvement between 2006 and 2008.

To examine poll worker confidence that the votes were counted accurately, we asked three separate confidence questions. First, we asked if the poll workers thought that the votes were counted accurately *in their voting location*. Second, we asked if the poll workers were confident that votes were counted correctly in other polling locations in their county. Third, we asked the poll workers if they were confident that the votes were counted accurately in other counties in New Mexico.

We ask these questions because the implementation of the election process is highly decentralized, and on Election Day, it is the poll workers who implement the election in precincts all across a given jurisdiction. These workers are, in many ways, the best people to evaluate the election process because (1) they can evaluate the experience at the polling place that others cannot easily observe, (2) they have been with other poll workers in training and have a sense of the quality of workers in other locations, and (3) they have a sense of the overall quality of the state laws and procedures that have to be implemented to make elections function well. Given the research on poll worker quality and their role in the voting process – and because they are in a position to evaluate that process – we ask these questions across multiple contexts.

At the level of the poll worker's voting location, there is a high level of confidence among the poll workers. Approximately 86 percent of the poll workers were very confident that the votes were counted accurately in their polling place. Santa Fe County was slightly above the overall average, at 94 percent. None of the poll workers sampled from San Juan County and Santa Fe Counties stated that they were "not very" or "not at all" confident that the votes in their polling place were counted accurately. In Bernalillo and Doña Ana counties, only 1.2 percent and 2.8 percent of poll workers, respectively, expressed that they were "not very" or "not at all" confident that the votes in their polling place were counted correctly.

These confidence percentages are much higher than what was reported in 2006. In 2006, only 57 percent of poll workers in Bernalillo County, 58 percent in Doña Ana County, and 75 percent in Santa Fe County indicated that they were "very confident" that the ballots in their voting location were counted correctly. The confidence levels in 2008 – in the 82 percent to 94 percent range – suggest more confidence in 2008 in the optical scan machines compared to 2006, when confidence was only between 57 percent and 75 percent. Because optical scan voting was first introduced in 2006 in New Mexico, the added poll worker experience with the optical scan machines may have created a higher comfort level with the machines that improved evaluations of poll worker confidence.

It is not surprising that poll workers might be confident that the ballots were counted correctly in their own precinct. After all, they are being asked if they have confidence in themselves. To tap into other aspects of confidence and allow us to determine how familiarity with the process influences attitudes about the election administration process more generally, we asked a second question: if the poll workers were confident that votes were counted accurately in other polling locations in their county. Here we see large differences in confidence across the counties. The San Juan County poll workers were the most confident that the votes in the other polling places in the county were counted accurately. The poll workers in Doña Ana County were least likely to answer that they were very confident that the votes in other precincts in the county were counted accurately; the most common answer in Doña Ana County was "somewhat confident."

Third, we asked the poll workers if they were confident that the votes were counted accurately in other counties in New Mexico. Across all of the counties, the most common answer among the poll workers across all four counties was that they were somewhat confident in vote-counting accuracy across other counties in New Mexico. Just under one-quarter (24%) of the poll workers said that they were very confident that the votes were counted accurately across the other counties.

Compared to New Mexico voters, whom we also surveyed, poll workers were much more confident that the votes in their polling place were counted accurately. Only 65 percent of voters, but nearly 9 in 10 poll workers, indicated that they were very confident that the votes in their polling place were counted accurately. However, when it came to confidence in vote counting in other precincts in the county and in other counties, this was not the case. Although many poll workers were still very confident and this was the most common response, many poll workers also opted for "don't know" in answer to this question, something that voters typically did not do. Even fewer poll workers, however, relative to voters indicated that they were not very confident or not confident at all.

Implementing Photo Identification Requirements

The use of surveys is also important for performance-based management in areas of importance related to implementation and service provisions. In elections, one such area is the way in which voters are authenticated at the polls. In all states, voters are required in some way to authenticate that they are eligible to vote, even if it just requires that they state their name to the poll worker so that it can be looked up on a voter roll.[7] Some states require that all voters show a valid form of government identification. In between are states, like New Mexico, that have laws that are a hybrid of these two extremes.

In the 2008 New Mexico general election, a voter could authenticate herself in the following ways:

- provide a verbal or written statement of her name, address, and year of birth
- show a physical form of identification, including an original or copy of a current and valid photo identification with or without an address (if there was an address, it did not have to match the voter rolls)
- show any of the following physical forms that include both a name and address (again, the address is not required to match the address that appears on the voter rolls): (1) utility bill, (2) bank statement, (3) government check, (4) paycheck, (5) student identification card, or (6) other government documents (e.g., ID issued by an Indian nation, tribe, or Pueblo)

In the survey, poll workers were asked how they asked voters to authenticate themselves, and in Table 4.7, we see the frequency and the average score of requests for different forms of identification. In these data (not shown in the table), we see significant differences between the answers given by presiding judges and poll clerks. Presiding judges were significantly more likely to ask for the correct identification (name, address, and birth year), significantly more likely to ask for proper identification from first-time voters who by law are supposed to provide additional identification, and significantly less likely to ask for ID for hearing reasons, to verify voter information. They were also more likely to ask voters to look up their numbers in the voter rolls.

---

[7] For those readers who think that North Dakota does not have such a list, see the state's election code.

TABLE 4.7. *Poll Workers Reported Use of Voter Identification Methods*

Way in Which Voter Was Authenticated	Very Often	Somewhat Often	Not Very Often	Not at All Often	Average
State name	65.2	15.1	9.7	10.0	3.4
State name and address	45.4	22.7	19.2	12.7	3.0
State name and birth year	29.6	20.3	26.7	23.4	2.6
State name, address, and birth year	27.6	16.8	26.6	29.0	2.4
Photo identification	16.6	19.4	35.1	28.9	2.2
Registration card	13.3	19.7	35.9	31.1	2.2
Had voters look up their number in rolls	7.6	11.1	23.3	58.0	1.7
None, knew the voter personally	4.4	8.4	18.1	69.1	1.5

Reasons for Requesting Voter Identification	Percentage Yes
Verify identity of first-time voters	59.2
Couldn't find the voter in the rolls	54.7
Verify identity of provisional voter	49.7
Information didn't match the voter rolls	38.3
It's required by law to verify the identity of voters	44.7
I did not recognize the voter	20.6
To prevent fraud	36.9
Trouble hearing/easier to read name from identification	20.5

The lack of consistency in the voter identification process is also confirmed by a follow-up question from the survey: "Did you ask a voter for any identification for any of the following reasons?" First-time voters by law have to provide identification that includes their address, so the fact that 59 percent of poll workers verified the identity of first-time voters is consistent with the law but also troubling, given that this means in 41 percent of cases, they did not authenticate voters who should have been authenticated. Moreover, it is troubling that nearly half of poll workers indicated that they were required by law to identify voters with a form of identification. All in-person voters must be authenticated verbally, but only first-time voters must be authenticated with physical identification. All of the other reasons to ask for identification are incorrect. For example, authenticating voters to "prevent fraud" is inappropriate, but over one-third (37%) of poll workers did so. Also, about one in five poll workers (21%) asked for identification because they could not hear well or because it was easier to read the voter's name from a physical form of identification.

Importantly, the preceding information corresponds to what we found in our voter surveys, thus providing further evidence that there were problems implementing voter identification law. Thus the method of triangulation and bringing multiple research strategies to the evaluation process provides additional evidence of a problem. However, while the poll worker data helped to define the problem generally, the voter surveys showed that the problem was more nuanced, with different types of voters (e.g., Hispanics and men) being treated differently than other types of voters (e.g., women and non-Hispanics).

When discrepancies in implementation are identified, survey data can also help managers determine why, in fact, such issues may have arisen. One important issue is whether there is a discriminatory component. In the New Mexico data, we find that minority poll workers – not white poll workers – were significantly more likely to ask for a physical form of ID across as many as eight of our voter identification variables. A second issue is whether there are partisan differences in implementation. Here the evidence is that poll workers who identify as being independents are the least likely to ask for alternative forms of identification, whereas Republicans are the most likely. For example, the average score for the photo identification request on the 5-point scale, with a higher number indicating more often, is 2.20 for Democrats, 2.31 for Republicans, and 2.19 for independents. Similarly, for the registration card identification, we see that the Democratic average is 2.12, the Republican average is 2.26, and the non–major party/independent average is 1.91. Thus there does appear to be some relationship between partisanship and voter identification requests. There is also a link between attitudes and behavior; poll workers who agree that photo identification should be required of each voter at the poll to prevent voter fraud are also significantly more likely to ask voters for photo identification (Atkeson et al. 2012).

The survey data also raise a question whether the training regarding photo identification was as effective as it should have been. Poll workers indicated that they were very well trained regarding what to ask for in terms of voter identification. Nearly 95 percent of poll workers indicated that "when to ask a voter for his or her identification before

voting" was very (72%) or somewhat (23%) clear, and only 5 percent indicated that it was not very clear (4%) or not at all clear (1%).
The training poll workers received appears to be inadequate, given the
variation seen in responses to the voter identification questions and the
workers' answers to questions on the poll worker survey. This led the
Bernalillo county Clerk Maggie Toulouse Oliver to develop a training
video that shows the correct way to implement voter identification.

Qualitative Measures of the Poll Worker Experience

The survey conducted in New Mexico is quite illustrative of the ways
in which poll workers can be surveyed to learn about the performance
of poll workers across many different metrics. Most beneficially, the
data from these surveys can be compared across elections and across
jurisdictions, allowing election officials to learn about how various
metrics change over time. However, sometimes election officials also
will want to obtain qualitative information from their poll workers.
They may want to understand the nuances of the implementation of a
new policy or new activity. Such information can often best be gathered
using qualitative analysis methods such as through focus groups.

An example of this type of analysis is a set of focus groups that
were done in Washington, D.C., for the district's board of elections in
2010 after the board implemented several reforms – including same-
day voter registration – in the primary election. The focus groups were
led by one of the authors over a three-day period after the primary
elections had concluded. The goal of the focus groups was to answer
three simple, but important, questions:

1. What problems did the poll workers experience in implementing
   the reforms in the 2010 primary election?
2. What solutions did they think would address the problems that
   they identified?
3. What were the largest concerns that they had for the upcoming
   general elections?

The data from this effort were beneficial for several reasons. First, the
primary election was September 14, 2010, leaving little time between it
and the November 2, 2010, general election, so the need for gathering
data immediately was strong. Thus a mail survey would not allow the

necessary turnaround time to obtain the surveys and do the analysis before the next election.[8] Second, the election officials knew some of the reasons why there had been problems in the election but wanted to collect systematic data on this topic. The focus groups used the same questions and addressed the same issues across all groups, allowing for the focus groups to collect a rigorous set of qualitative data from the poll workers. Third, the narratives provided by the poll workers in the focus groups provided details regarding the problems that arose in the election.

One key issue that arose in the focus groups was that there was an interaction between the partisan primary election – where many voters had issues associated with their party identification and eligibility to vote in a closed primary election – and same-day voters, who also were being helped at the same table as voters with problems with their partisan registrations. If a survey had just asked about lines related to same-day registration, the poll workers might not have differentiated between these voters and voters with problems with their partisan registrations, both of which are voters with special needs but different types of needs.

The focus groups also identified specific issues that occurred related to the need for cross-training poll workers so that they could work multiple jobs on Election Day. Washington, D.C., has historically trained poll workers to work a single job in the election, but the precinct captains wanted to be able to move poll workers around based on demands that arose such as having long lines of special-needs voters. The poll workers also identified weaknesses with the technology and processes used to process special-needs voters. The Washington, D.C., Board of Election was able to change the processes and improve the technology used so that the general election proceeded more smoothly.

Conclusions

Given the importance of poll workers in elections, getting their feedback is critical to the performance-based management process. Election officials can use poll worker surveys for an array of metrics – from

---

[8] Of course, phone surveys of poll workers would be another option but would cost a great deal more.

problems at the polls to issues associated with training. Moreover, these data can be triangulated with voter surveys, incident reports, and other data to identify management problems that may have arisen in the election. For example, in the New Mexico case, part of the problem with the voter identification law implementation was that many of the poll workers did not understand the law and therefore did not know how to implement it. This suggests a problem in training, which can be remedied through revamping the training.

Another benefit of evaluating poll workers is that it provides election officials a window into understanding the demographic characteristics of poll workers and if their poll workers are reflective of the population at large. Descriptive representation is an important aspect of public administration, and voters are sensitive to these characteristics, as Hall and Stewart (2011) have found. Many states also have laws governing the political representation of poll workers, requiring a mix of Democrats and Republicans in the polls. The surveys provide information to the election officials about these important attributes of poll workers.

One interesting aspect of surveying poll workers is that they are generally very inclined to provide feedback on the process. Whether critiquing the quality of training, evaluating their colleagues, or reporting successes and failures at the polls, poll workers are an easy source of data about the voting process. Election officials can build metrics about polling place performance around these surveys and then track changes in performance over time, comparing different clusters of poll workers who work together.

5

Auditing the Election Ecosystem

Election administration is a highly complex process that involves multiple actors all working to achieve the goal of running an effective election.[1] Accomplishing this goal requires election officials coordinating the efforts of contractors (from ballot printers to voting machine companies), third parties (like the U.S. Postal Service, which transports absentee ballots, and the entities that agree to house polling places), and the poll workers who actually implement the election at the polls. Managing this vast enterprise of actors within the organization and across a network of outside actors requires election officials to evaluate their election activities so that they can improve the implementation of the process over time (O'Toole and Meier 1999).

One important way to gather the performance data needed to improve election management is through an election ecosystem audit (EEA).[2] These audits are evaluations of an election from start to finish that especially emphasize the administrative aspects of the election process.[3] This type of evaluation uses both existing data that are collected as a matter of course in the election process and new data that are specifically generated for this purpose. Postelection voting machine performance audits – where the original count of the election is

[1] Alvarez and Hall (2006).
[2] This type of auditing is discussed in detail in Alvarez, Atkeson, and Hall (2012).
[3] E.g., see Atkeson et al. (2008a).

compared with a postelection hand count of ballots – is an example of this latter type.[4]

As we have argued throughout this book, quite a lot of data are generated over the course of an election, but much of these data are never used for evaluative purposes. However, these data provide useful information about the quality of the election and should feed into the election management process. This would allow election officials, stakeholders, and researchers to carefully examine the data to improve the process for the next election. Training, procedures, and processes can be modified to address shortfalls that were identified during the EEA. Thus the point of an EEA is to provide a feedback mechanism to improve the performance of local election administration.

The following steps are designed to show how an ecosystem audit works. These audits require planning but also provide quite effective data for improving election management. The analysis of this audit process comes from our research on election evaluation audits in New Mexico and Utah. In this process, we give special attention to post-election machine performance audits, which have been mandated by statute in many states over the last several years. Postelection ballot audits (PEBA) serve two purposes. First, they help to verify the performance of voting systems and to varying degrees ensure that the election outcomes are correct. This check can also serve as a mechanism for detecting potential fraud in the election (e.g., Alvarez et al. 2008a, chapters 9–11). Second, they provide data for process improvement; for example, they can identify how voters interact with technology and the voting process to determine where discrepancies exist between voter intention and machine counting. Broadly speaking, PEBAs are

---

[4] E.g., see M. Halvorson and L. Wolff (for Citizens for Election Integrity Minnesota), "Report and Analysis of the 2006 Post-election Audit of Minnesota's Voting Systems," http://electionaudits.org/files/MN%20Audit%20Report%20by%20CEIMN.pdf; P. Smith (for VerifiedVoting.org), "Written Testimony before Committee on House Administration, Subcommittee on Elections," U.S. House of Representatives, http://electionaudits.org/files/PamelaSmithTestimonyFinal_2007mar20.pdf; "Case Study: Auditing the Vote," http://electionline.org/Portals/1/Publications/EB17.pdf; S. Cohen, "Auditing Technology for Electronic Voting Machines," VTP Working Paper 46, 2005, http://www.votingtechnologyproject.org/wps-recent.html; S. Popoveniuc and B. Hosp, "An Introduction to Punchscan," http://punchscan.org/papers/popoveniuc_hosp_punchscan_introduction.pdf.

becoming a more common practice across states to ensure election integrity and instill voter confidence.[5]

There is a great deal of variation across states in when audits are triggered and how they are conducted. For example, some states have requirements for PEBAs that are triggered only when certain events occur such as a close election or a clear problem with ballot counting. Some states have election audit requirements that are only required for electronic voting but not for optical scan or other paper ballots. California and several other states require that a certain percentage of all ballots be audited each election, and New Mexico uses a risk-limiting audit methodology, in which the number of ballots and machines recounted varies based on the outcome of the election and the number of ballots cast. Another common variation is in the number and type of contests audited. Some states audit the entire ballot, but other states only audit certain contests, especially statewide races.

In most states, PEBAs are relatively limited in scope, and election officials are typically the individuals who are required to conduct the audits of their own actions. Only in Washington State does a third party, the county auditor, conduct the audit. Having a third party conduct audits is a best practice in audits, as noted by the Government Accountability Office and other standard-setting bodies (Alvarez et al. 2012). Interestingly, half of the states that implement audits do not require that the results be formally reported. Even in states with reporting requirements, the state may not issue a formal report that details all of the audit results and any problems that were identified. Given these wide variations in implementation and practice, we make recommendations on procedural practices for conducting postelection audits later in this chapter.

What Is an Election Ecosystem Audit?

Although PEBAs are critical for election administration, so critical that we have recently edited a volume of essays on the topic of PEBAs (see Alvarez et al. 2012), they are only a part of a broader EEA. A

[5] http://www.verifiedvoting.org/.

complete EEA will audit the entire election administration process, from start to finish, and as a consequence, the EEA will provide a great deal of helpful evaluative data. A well-done EEA is no substitute for an ecosystem study, but the information gathered from the EEA should factor directly into ecosystems analysis. In the rest of this chapter, we discuss the important steps in an EEA and then delineate how the results of the EEA can fit into an election ecosystems analysis.

Steps in an Election Ecosystem Audit

There are eight steps to an ecosystem audit. It starts with mapping the entire election process – from logic and accuracy testing through end-of-election ballot counting – and then requires evaluating various processes and activities throughout the election.

Step 1: Mapping the Election Process

The first key step in conducting an EEA is to map out each aspect of the election process. This requires thinking about each step in the process of running the election; it is quite helpful to flowchart these activities. It is also important to identify the forms and reports that are produced through the election process that can be used to document the completion of each task. The flowcharting process will identify all key players in the election process, delineate the various steps in the registration and voting process, and identify potential breaks in the chain of custody process that will make auditing the election more difficult.

For example, in Figure 5.1, we show a flowchart for the absentee voting process in Davis County, Utah. It starts with ballots being ordered and then checked for accuracy. Various logging procedures – such as adding bar codes to ballots and tracking which voters received absentee ballots – are noted. The process of the ballot leaving the custody of the election official is noted, and the procedures used to process returned ballots are noted. This flowchart is actually simple and leaves out some steps that might be important such as the method by which ballots are transferred to the U.S. Postal Service. It does, however, cover almost all of the important activities in a typical absentee voting process.

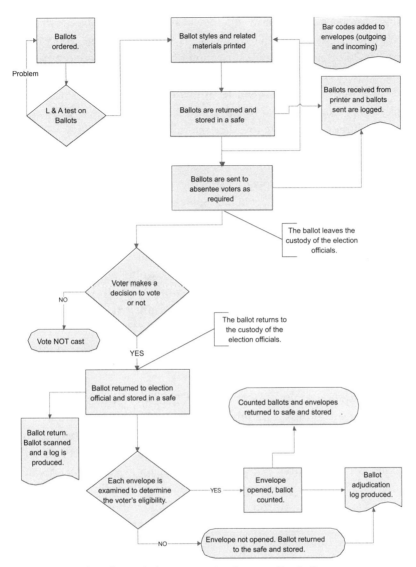

FIGURE 5.1. Flowchart of Absentee Voting Process, Davis County

Step 2: Auditing Each Process

Elections have an array of processes that occur before the election that should be observed and examined to ensure that the process is being completed correctly. For example, all states have some law or regulation related to logic and accuracy testing. This is the first process that can be mapped: how do the local election officials test these machines, and what documentation is produced at the end of this process? For example, a local election official might produce a signed checklist at the end of the process showing how an electronic tabulator (for optical scan or direct recording electronic (DRE) voting) was physically examined and tested for its tabulation accuracy. The logic and accuracy test needs to cover the tabulation technology used for early voting, absentee voting, and in-person precinct voting.

Furthermore, the training of election workers is also critical, given the key role that they play as street-level bureaucrats implementing election policy (e.g., Hall et al. 2008; Hall and Stewart 2011). An audit of any type generally has a strong focus on training and personnel and how people are taught to implement processes. Training documents, the manuals poll workers have to reference at the polls on Election Day, and the issues emphasized in training would all be examined in an EEA. The processes of training poll workers of all types should be mapped, and training materials should be evaluated. These evaluative exercises, when combined with other performance data, such as polling place incident reports, poll worker and voter surveys, and observation analyses, will help identify places where training can be improved for the next election cycle.

It is also important to audit each voting mode – absentee, early, and Election Day voting – carefully because the same activity conducted in a different election mode may have different steps and different procedures. These audits focus on ballot reconciliation, chain of custody issues, and procedures. For absentee voting, audits are critical because election officials lose physical custody of the ballot while it is in transit in the mail to and from the voter. An audit should allow for the accounting of where and when ballots were sent to the voter, when ballots were returned to the local election official, and how the ballots were handled and secured at the local election official site before and after counting. For absentee voting, an EEA might include (1) auditing the physical location where the ballots are stored for security and privacy, (2) accounting to ensure that the number of ballots printed minus the number of ballots sent out equals the number of unsent ballots, (3) the procedures for challenging and rejecting absentee ballots, and (4) whether the number of absentee votes in the election is similar to previous patterns of absentee voting.

This part of the audit might also include a review of the mailing process to ensure efficiency and accuracy in the process. For example, in 2008 in New Mexico, snafus in getting ballots mailed out on time so that voters could return them on time led to a larger than normal number of ballots that were not returned.[6] Reviewing this process to determine why ballots were not mailed out in a timely manner might result in changes in administration of the program within the organization, a reconfiguration of the process to make it more efficient, or the hiring of new, or more, staff. Tackling issues that created immediate problems during the election is a smart way to improve the process for the next election.

Another problem in a different county in New Mexico in 2008 was that the U.S. Postal Service returned absentee voter ballot packages back to the county instead of sending them to the voter. In this case, the postal service was processing some of the absentee ballot envelopes upside down, as if the return address to the clerk's office on the back of the outer envelope was the actual mailing address. The county clerk had to intervene and discuss the issue with the local postmaster. The moral of the story is that future preparations for absentee ballot voters should consider how the U.S. Postal Service processes mailings and how that affects the efficient mailing of election material.

For early voting, a critical issue is being able to account for the security and custody of ballots over the entire early voting period and reconciling this with the number of individuals who cast ballots. An EEA of the early voting process might include (1) examining whether the total number of voters who signed the voter registry on a given day equals the number of voters who cast ballots on that same day, (2) if the total number of votes cast and the total number of voters in one day provide the starting number for the number of votes cast and the number of voters who have voted in the next day, and (3) a review of any logs that are kept showing how the chain of custody of the voting system was maintained each day.

Another key process to study is provisional balloting, a key fail-safe mechanism in the electoral process. An EEA of this process

[6] Key Duhigg (2009), "Count Every Vote New Mexico 2008 Election Report," Common Cause Typescript, http://www.commoncause.org/site/pp.asp?c=dkLNK1MQIwG&b=4847593 .

might examine (1) how many provisional ballots were cast, (2) if any precincts have more provisional ballots than would be expected based on data from other precincts or past history, (3) the processes and procedures for determining whether a provisional ballot is qualified, (4) the number of ballots that were counted and rejected, and (5) the primary reasons for rejection. These data can be used to improve training, processes, and procedures in future elections. For example, if the EEA identifies a high number of provisional ballots being rejected because poll workers are failing to complete the outside of the provisional balloting envelope correctly, this would lead to a management recommendation to improve poll worker training and standard operating procedures for processing such ballots on Election Day.

Finally, the most important yet generally overlooked issue in thinking about elections from an EEA standpoint is voter registration. Voter registration files are the foundation of the voting process; if you are not correctly registered, you typically cannot vote. These files must have integrity and therefore should be audited for accuracy. A basic issue for such an audit is whether it should be a 100 percent audit of the file or an audit of a sample of the file. A 100 percent audit examines the file completely, but this is costly, time consuming, and human resource intensive. An alternative is to conduct an audit of a sample of the voter registration file. A sample could identify the most problematic areas and where to focus energies to improve quality. In either case, a registration audit may consider the following facets of voter registration:

1. Data on third-party registrants could be examined carefully to look for conformity with the law and for delivery and input of newly registered voters. More efficient processes for handling voter registration forms during the stress of an election cycle might improve efficiency and general management.
2. Data on provisional voting can be used to help audit the voter registration files. This is especially true if a problem with the file is the cause of a provisional vote.
3. Incident reports may also be used to identify voter registration problems.[7]

---

[7] See Kiewiet et al. (2008), for a discussion of how to use incident reports for this purpose.

4. Survey data – of voters and poll workers – may provide additional data about the voter's experience with voter registration and problems at the polls on Election Day.

Step 3: Election Day Voting

Election Day is still when most Americans cast ballots. Because of this, it should be a central focus of any EEA. The EEA audit of the in-person Election Day voting process can use logs of security tags and seals, incident reports, rovers from the central office, and information from third-party election observers to identify problems at the polling place. These problems may include (1) problems related to opening or closing the polls, (2) a lack of necessary supplies, (3) reconciliation of ballots (the total ballots cast at the end of the day equals the number of voters who signed in to vote), (4) issues related to the polling place, (5) voter privacy issues, and (6) a lack of consistency in procedures across precincts (e.g., handling of voter identification or handling of provisional voters). For example, auditing of closing procedures might produce information on where poll workers get confused in reconciliation and result in better instructions for the next election.

Step 4: EEA and Special Populations

Jurisdictions with sizable special populations – such as language minorities or overseas and military voters – should take special care to audit the processes used by these populations to register and vote. For example, in jurisdictions covered by the language minority provisions of the Voting Rights Act, an audit would likely include examining the translated materials used to assist language minority voters and evaluating the quality of the interpreter services provided to these voters. Likewise, it might be important to interview language minority voters using an exit poll or interest groups that work with these voters to ensure that voters were not pressured or given improper assistance by these interpreters.

In the case of overseas or military voters, examining the ballots that were or were not included in the final tally of votes and the reasons why votes were or were not rejected would be important. An audit conducted after the 2000 election in Florida identified myriad issues associated with the determination of whether to include or exclude this category of ballots in the final canvass, and a study of absentee voting in Los Angeles County identified problems associated with military and overseas voters having their ballots returned in time to be counted.[8]

Step 5: A Postelection Ballot Audit

The PEBA provides a final check on the chain of custody procedures used in the election and ensures that the initial count on Election Day was not flawed for some reason (e.g., fraud, poor logic and accuracy testing of tabulation software). Audits can be *hot*, completed before certification of the voting results, or *cold*, completed after certification of the election. Hot audits are preferred by some election activists because they are completed before the results are certified. Theoretically, the results from a hot audit could be used to overturn the results of an election that was found to have fraudulent results.

In the following, we consider how to conduct a PEBA for optical scan ballots and for ballots cast on a DRE voting machine:

1. *Organizing the ballots.* Regardless of the unit of analysis for the audit (ballot, precinct, or some other batch unit), some amount of ballot organization will be needed. For example, New Mexico's PEBA samples precincts, and so absentee and in-person early ballots have to be sorted after (in the case of early voters) or before (for absentee by mail voters) ballot tallying into their prospective precincts. With DRE voting with a paper trail, the paper tapes will need to be organized onto a spool or other mechanism that allows the paper tape to be reviewed easily.

2. *Transparency.* Transparency and openness are critical for any postelection audit process. To the extent possible, all steps and aspects of any postelection audit process must be open to public input and observation, and the results of all postelection audits should be made easily available to the interested public.

3. *Audit team selection.* A competent, independent, and effective audit team is required to perform the audit efficiently and accurately. Independence of the team members, especially the audit manager, is necessary to ensure that the auditor is free from conflicts of interest and external threats to independence. Counting

---

[8] See, e.g., Wolter et al. (2003) and Alvarez et al. (2008a).

and administrative team members need to have good counting and focus skills.

4. *Sampling of voting systems for audit.* The process of sampling of voting systems should be transparent, open to public participation, and use stratified random sampling, stratified by the local jurisdictional unit. Thus sampling should include all jurisdictional units and all voting modes.[9] It is necessary to include all jurisdictions because jurisdictional units are largely responsible for the logic and accuracy testing of their machines, and so if there is a problem with a machine, it is likely specific to a jurisdictional unit and may suggest larger problems for them. It is necessary to include all voting modes because each voting mode has different potential security and voting threats that have to be accounted for by the local election official. County election officials should consider oversampling voting systems when they have reasons to think that there might have

---

[9] See, e.g., A. W. Appel, "Effective Audit Policy for Voter-Verified Paper Ballots," Center for Information Technology Policy/Department of Computer Science, Princeton University, http://www.cs.princeton.edu/~appel/papers/appel-audits.pdf; J. A. Calandrino, J. A. Halderman, and E. W. Felten, "In Defense of Pseudorandom Sample Selection," USENIX/ACCURATE Electronic Voting Technology Workshop 2008, http://www.usenix.org/event/evto8/tech/full_papers/calandrino/calandrino.pdf; A. Cordero, D. Wagner, and D. Dill, "The Role of Dice in Election Audits – Extended Abstract," IAVoSS Workshop on Trustworthy Elections 2006 (WOTE 2006), http://www.cs.berkeley.edu/~daw/papers/dice-wote06.pdf; J. L. Hall, "Research Memorandum: On Improving the Uniformity of Randomness with Alameda County's Random Selection Process," UC Berkeley School of Information, http://josephhall.org/papers/alarand_memo.pdf; J. McCarthy, H. Stanislevic, M. Lindeman, A. Ash, V. Addona, and M. Batcher, "Percentage-Based versus SAFE Vote Tabulation Auditing: A Graphic Comparison," http://www.verifiedvotingfoundation.org; L. Norden, A. Burstein, J. Lorenzo Hall, and M. Chen, "Post-election Audits: Restoring Trust in Elections," http://www.brennancenter.org/content/resource/post_election_audits_restoring_trust_in_elections_executive_summary/; Post-Election Audit Standards Working Group, "Evaluation of Audit Sampling Models and Options for Strengthening California's Manual Count," http://www.sos.ca.gov/elections/elections_peas.htm; R. Rivest, "On Auditing Elections When Precincts Have Different Sizes," VTP Working Paper 55, http://www.votingtechnologyproject.org/wps-recent.html; R. Rivest and R. Popa, "On Estimating the Size and Confidence of a Statistical Audit," VTP Working Paper 54, http://www.votingtechnologyproject.org/wps-recent.html; H. Stanislevic, "NY Election Audits: Is Three Percent Enough?" E-Voter Education Project; P. Stark, "Conservative Statistical Post-election Audits," http://uscountvotes.net/docs_pdf/info/US/StarkconservativeElectionAudits07.pdf.

been some sort of problem involving those voting systems. It is preferable that the sampling occur very late on Election Day or postelection. If precincts are selected prior to the election, any effort to subvert the system can avoid these precincts. If precincts are selected after the election, there may be a bias toward selecting "good precincts," although completely public and transparent random sampling should limit these concerns.

5. *Chain of custody procedures.* All counties should develop chain of custody procedures for their postelection audits and make them available to the public. Chain of custody procedures should emphasize security of the ballots and the election process. Ballots counted by hand need to be accounted for at every stage of the postelection auditing process. Thus counters must confirm at every stage that they are receiving or returning the correct number of ballots.

6. *Audit forms and logs.* Develop audit forms for the postelection audit to facilitate a smooth audit process and provide quick results to the public on completion. These include a log of the Election Day machine count as provided by the poll workers and judges for each counting machine and the hand-count audit forms for the postelection audit. Also, it is important for the integrity of the process to develop a log and a procedure for hand counters to check out and return ballots during the audit period.

7. *Voter intent standards.* Election officials should develop precise voter intent standards based on state law, and these voter intent standards should be communicated to audit team members as part of their training.

8. *Hand-counting procedures.* An audit supervisor should be placed in charge of the audit to coordinate and facilitate the hand count in a timely and efficient manner, monitor and train the counting team(s), summarize the findings and provide that information to the county clerk, and maintain chain of custody rules over the course of the audit. Counting teams should not have any information about the totals from the machine counts to prevent the appearance of coercion or influence of readers and counters in their count. Counting teams should have a minimum of two people: one counter and one reader.

9. *Reporting.* The results of the audit should be released as soon as possible after completing the audit on the county clerk's Web site or other public place if a Web site is not available and should be provided to the secretary of state. The secretary of state should report individual county-level results on the secretary of state's Web site. Both files should be downloadable for public examination. The results should show the total number of ballots recorded by machine, the total number of votes cast for each candidate by machine, the parallel data from the hand count, and the percentage difference between the machine and hand counts.

10. *Handling problems.* Additional procedures should be developed for problems found over the course of the audit so they can be resolved.

PEBAs are primarily about creating confidence and assurance that the election outcomes are accurate. However, they can also provide other valuable information about the election ecosystem. For example, in the New Mexico audit pilot project (Atkeson et al. 2008a, 2008b), the research team found that there was an increase in overvotes on the no-contest yes–no vote for state and local judges. The ballot design for these contests was substantially different than for other contests on the ballot. This suggests that a ballot design change may enhance the voter's voting experience and create more efficiency for the voter and for the processing of ballots.

Step 6: Archiving of All Audit Material

All forms, counts, and other data generated by all aspects of the audit, especially the postelection machine performance audit, should be archived for future reference in case of litigation and to provide a history of the election process that can be reviewed by the public, elected officials, or other interested parties. We recommend that these should be centralized for easy access, though election jurisdictions likely will also want to keep a copy for their internal record keeping as well. One possible location for these materials would be the state library. Libraries already maintain procedures for examining state documents and thus provide an obvious and accessible storage place for these valuable materials. State library storage also relieves the burden on the secretary of state's office, or other state offices that oversee elections, from maintaining these materials and providing rules for their public access.

Step 7: Reporting and Transparency

For an EEA to be maximally effective, all the procedures and steps involved need to be highly transparent. In practice, that means announcing when various steps of an EEA will be conducted to the public well in advance of their implementation. Transparency also requires that the public be allowed to observe the stages of an EEA in person and online.

All of the results of the EEA need to be made public. Reports of how each step was conducted, the data from the EEA, and all summary reports should be released for public comment and dissemination. Again, the stakeholders need to know how the EEA was conducted and be able to see all the results from the EEA for it to be effective in helping to ensure the integrity of an election administration process.

Also, the EEA results integrate well with an overall analysis of the elections ecosystem. A thorough EEA will produce results that, if corroborated with other studies of the same election administrative process, will help to establish priorities for change and reform. Anomalous results from an EEA may point to areas that need additional study; for example, audits of a voter registration system that find a high number of duplicates might lead the election administrator to seek a more thorough study of the voter registration database in question or how voter registration applications are received and entered. But this integration with a thorough election administration ecosystems analysis will best be established if the EEA is done in a transparent and public manner.

Conclusions

Over the past several years, a segment of the election advocate community has become increasingly interested in election audits but has become specifically fixated on the postelection comparison of hand-counted ballots to the electronic results that occur on Election Day. Largely, this fixation comes from concerns from many in the advocacy community about potential issues with the quality of the electronic software and hardware used for ballot casting (in the case of DREs) and ballot tabulation (in the case of both DREs and optically scanned ballots). By comparing the postelection hand count of paper to the electronic count, these audits hope to catch any problems in the balloting process and any errors with the tabulation software.

These postelection count audits are a necessary part of the auditing process, but – as we have argued in this chapter – they are not sufficient for ensuring that elections are free from problems, including problems that can affect vote tabulation. A postelection audit assumes that all of the inputs into that audit – the ballots, the machines – are the same ones that were used in the election; it assumes that a chain of custody exists. An EEA includes a postelection audit, but it also includes an audit of all processes and procedures that lead up to that audit. This means that other problems – such as problems with whether to include provisional ballots in the count or problems with voter registration that may have kept certain individuals from voting (or required them to vote provisionally) – will be captured in an EEA but not in a pure postelection ballot count audit. These other problems can be more severe, and there is some evidence that they are more common, than problems with the postelection count.

In addition, the point of an EEA is not merely to collect data about the performance of the system at various parts of the election process; instead, the audit should result in a set of management recommendations that identify weaknesses in the system that should be addressed in the future as well as a set of strengths in the system that should be maintained. This will allow the local election official to know how to improve the election process in that jurisdiction. The EEA process should result in a stronger system in the future and an improved set of standard operating procedures that govern the election. It also provides the election officials with important information that they need to be able to communicate with key constituencies – the media, policy makers, voters, and their internal staff and external implementation network – about how any given election performed. This communication provides important transparency and avoids possible questions about certain aspects of the voting process.

6

Election Observation

So far, we have focused on the use of quantitative data to study election system performance: voter and poll worker surveys, studies of residual votes, and how such data can be used for performance-based management. In this chapter, we turn to an entirely different source of data, but one that is critical for determining electoral performance. Here we focus on direct personal examination of an election by trained observers.

Election observation is a type of qualitative data analysis; collection of these data normally focuses on a relatively small number of precincts that are studied closely and intensely. It is qualitative because it relies primarily on the eyes and ears of observers and on their perceptions, intuition, and experience. It is qualitative because what observers focus on in one precinct might differ dramatically from what they might focus on in another precinct. Although all of this can make qualitative data difficult to analyze in a systematic manner, it does not mean that qualitative analysis of election performance by observers is inferior to other types of data analysis. This also does not mean that no systematic data are collected during the process. Indeed, we advise that the collection of qualitative, observational data includes some more systematic components.

Election observation is a critical tool for election performance measurement for a number of reasons. First, direct personal observations often allow the study of things that might not occur to the researcher before the election – things that might not make it onto a voter or poll worker survey but might be noticed by an election observer. This is particularly important in situations where procedures or technology has changed, and it might not be clear when or how problems might arise. Second, observers are in a situation to place things in their context. Thus occurrences that on paper might sound problematic to a researcher might have a particular context that explains why they happen. Third, direct observation is particularly important for studying how voters and poll workers interact and for determining how a polling location affects the poll workers and voters in that location.

Collectively, we have engaged in direct, personal election observation in many counties in a number of states as well as internationally. We have worked on observation efforts that were closely controlled by others, especially election officials. But we have also worked on observation projects that we controlled completely, which gave us substantial flexibility as researchers. Most important for our purposes in this chapter, we have conducted large-scale election observation efforts in the 2006, 2008, and 2010 general elections in New Mexico, and the lessons we learned from those experiences provide us with the framework for this chapter.

A Brief History of Election Observation

Today, when an election is held outside the United States, it is common for that election to be observed and studied by foreign representatives associated with a variety of different international organizations. For example, the Organization for Security and Cooperation in Europe maintains an Office for Democratic Institutions and Human Rights (ODIHR), and representatives from the ODIHR frequently observe elections around the world. Other organizations, like the Carter Center, also have election monitoring observation programs: as of April 2009, the Carter Center had monitored 75 elections in 29 countries, beginning in 1989. Although international election monitoring teams commonly work in newly forming democratic nations, they also are frequently present in long-standing democracies. ODIHR often studies elections held in Europe, for instance, and, in 2008, was present in the United States.[1]

---

[1] See http://www.osce.org/odihr and http://www.cartercenter.org/peace/democracy/index.html.

This was not always the case, as prior to 1962, there were no recorded cases of formal election observation missions (Hyde 2008). In the past few decades, the practice of international election monitoring has become quite common, especially in newly developing democracies. Many of the organizations that undertake these efforts have developed elaborate and well-tested methodologies for implementation of an election observation process in virtually all election contexts.[2] The explosion in election monitoring efforts has recently spawned a small, but growing, academic research literature on how election monitoring works and on the effects that it might have on detecting and deterring election manipulation (see Bjornlund 2004; Hyde 2010; Simpser 2008).

In this book, we are focused primarily on the United States, and given that context, we need to make two important points for readers familiar with the American election process. First, when we discuss election observers or monitors, we always are assuming that these observers or monitors (we will use those terms interchangeably) are independent of both those administering the election and those who have candidates or issues at stake in the election. In the United States, there is a tradition in some states and localities of having partisan poll watchers in polling places to monitor election activities in an attempt to ensure that representatives of both major parties can observe and potentially intervene in the voting process should problems be identified.[3] For an unbiased election observation process, it is critical that the observers be nonpartisan and independent of both those administering the election and those with a stake in the outcome of that election.

Second, the election laws and regulations in most states are either silent about independent observers or may not permit them easy access to polling sites on Election Day. As the Commission on Federal Election Reform (2005, 65) noted in its report, when it discussed the importance of allowing nonpartisan and independent election observers, "only one of our 50 states (Missouri) allows unfettered access to polling stations

---

[2] There are some exceptions, in particular, in recent elections, as many of these organizations have begun to grapple with the question of how to observe elections in which electronic voting technologies are widely used.

[3] A recent law review article discusses both the history and legal status of partisan poll watchers (Heidelbaugh et al. 2009).

by international observers. The election laws of the other 49 states either lack any reference to international observers or fail to include international observers in the statutory categories of persons permitted to enter polling places." This introduces an important problem for independent election observers in the American context, a problem that we wanted to point out here and that we discuss in more detail in this chapter.

Some General Considerations for Developing Election Observation Studies

As we discussed in previous chapters, it is critical that any election observation effort start with the identification of the basic research questions that need to be answered. The research questions should be specific; for example, the team might be interested in looking at the precise implementation of a particular new procedure or regulation like a photo identification requirement. Or the question might be whether polling places are laid out to accommodate the flow of voters or to see if they meet requirements for accessibility for individuals with disabilities.

One way to develop research questions is to consider recent legal and regulatory changes as well as procedures that are complicated or potentially discriminatory. Concerns raised in news stories or by election officials in recent elections may also provide guidance. Questions may also arise from participating in local poll worker training. Because election law and custom vary a great deal across jurisdictions and especially states, we recommend that, whenever possible, election observers attend poll worker training to understand how the local election officials implement the laws, rules of administration, chain of custody, and other election procedures. In addition, this provides another area of examination and potential recommendations for improvements.

Armed with clear research questions, the team then needs to develop a clear and consistent data collection instrument. Although election observation is an inherently qualitative activity, it is also an opportunity for the collection of uniform and consistent quantitative data. Important data elements would include the polling place location, the date and time of the observation, the observers, and a place to record

any anomalous observations. The form would also include standardized questions that focus on the research questions identified by the
researchers such as basic questions regarding precinct accessibility or
regarding the implementation of photo identification procedures. Standardized data collection instruments help observers in the field focus
on certain aspects of the election effort they see in front of them
and help force them to look at certain aspects of the process in a
systematic way.

Once the research questions are clear and an observation instrument
is developed, the researchers then have to determine where to deploy
observation teams. This will depend to some extent on resources and
on the research problems at hand. An election observation effort with
substantial resources and research problems that are not geographic
in nature might want to deploy the observation teams in a random
manner. Random selection can be an effective way to gain widespread
coverage of an election. However, an election observation effort that
has fewer resources, or has research questions that are in some way
geographically constrained, might wish to target the observation teams
to carefully chosen locations.

Observation team members need to be carefully recruited and well
trained. Anyone who will be sent into the field must have the appropriate personal and professional skills to be an effective field researcher.
This may mean having certain necessary language skills or, in some situations, a certain racial, ethnic, demographic, or cultural background.
At a minimum, it is necessary that field researchers be sensitive to
all political, racial, ethnic, cultural, or religious factors that might be
operative in the field research project in addition to the rules and election procedures. It is also important that all those who will be in the
field understand the research goals, that they understand the correct
and appropriate regulations and procedures governing the election,
that they be trained in how to collect the required data, and that
they be briefed regarding how to respond to anomalous situations.
Detailed training of any researchers who are going into the field is
imperative as they need to be instructed clearly on the ground rules
for their fieldwork. For example, research team members who are sent
to study polling places on Election Day need to be trained on how
to inform local election officials about their presence, where they can
be stationed in a polling place, whether they can approach voters or

others in or outside the polling place, and what intervention strategies exist. Most critically, field researchers need to understand that they are observers – not participants – and that, as observers, they should have an open mind as they observe. People may come to the research project with certain views about something being observed – such as regarding photo identification – but these views should not be allowed to affect the observation project.

Finally, election observation studies should be developed with some flexibility in mind, and the research team ought to have in place some means to communicate with each observation team. Those leading the research effort must have contingency plans for last-minute changes in the research plan to deal with any new problems or potential malfeasance that may arise at the last minute. For example, having an observational team leader who is the central contact for all observation team members is helpful to bringing new information into the observational loop. Phone trees can be developed to create efficiency in communicating information that may assist in assessing implementation of election procedures. However, exactly how flexibility can be implemented is contingent on the research question, the political and electoral situation, and the research methodology. For example, if prior information leads the research leaders to concentrate Election Day field observers in a certain geographic part of a jurisdiction, the research leaders should either have a means to reallocate the field observers to other locations if new information indicates problems or malfeasance in another geographic location or perhaps have some field teams in reserve so that they can be assigned to the places where new problems or potential malfeasance arise.

In the next section of this chapter, we discuss our election monitoring efforts in New Mexico and some of the important issues involved in developing an effective election monitoring study. We follow up by discussing some of the lessons we learned from those efforts.

New Mexico 2006, 2008, and 2010 Election Observation Methodology

In the 2006 New Mexico general elections, teams of observers examined Election Day voting operations in three New Mexico counties (Bernalillo, Doña Ana, and Santa Fe counties). For this project, the county clerks provided the research teams with full and independent access to every precinct in the county. In addition, the research teams were allowed to monitor and observe precinct operations for as long as team members deemed necessary and were allowed to return to precincts multiple times over the course of the day. Thus the research teams had freedom of mobility and no restrictions, other than following good rules of behavior, on their activities.

Because the 2006 observation methodology worked well – and to have as much comparability as possible with this project – the research team adopted a very similar methodology for monitoring the 2008 presidential election. This comparability allowed the researchers to assess both the current election administration performance and how procedural, administrative, and legal changes implemented since 2006 may have affected the performance of the electoral system in 2008.

The important policy change made prior to the 2006 election was that the state adopted the use of optical scan voting for use in all counties. This voting technology requires a voter to fill in a bubble next to the name of a candidate as a means of marking her vote choice. If a voter votes through the absentee voting process, these ballots are tabulated centrally using the Election Systems and Software (ES&S) Model 650 (M650) ballot tabulator in larger counties and the ES&S Model 100 (M100) in smaller counties. For voters casting ballots in early or Election Day voting in a precinct, these ballots are tabulated using the ES&S M100 tabulator. In addition, voters with special needs can use the ES&S AutoMARK, which allows the voter to make vote choices using an electronic touch screen interface. These choices are then printed onto a paper ballot that can be scanned into either the M100 or M650 tabulator.

The research teams did, however, make a number of improvements to the 2008 study and expanded its scope relative to the 2006 study. Three important changes in 2008 relative to 2006 were in the scope of the election observation efforts:

- First, the scope of the study was expanded to cover early and absentee voting as those two methods of casting ballots are increasingly utilized in New Mexico.[4] This required having observers study

---

[4] In 2008, early voting was the highest ever reported, with 38% of all ballots cast using this voting mode. Twenty-one percent of voters chose to vote absentee, and

these two processes in the days before and after the 2008 general election.

- Second, the scope of the study was expanded to include another New Mexican county, San Juan County. This provided an opportunity to study the implementation of New Mexico's election regulations in a different context than was considered in the 2006 study.
- Third, the study was expanded to include additional precincts in the counties studied on Election Day. This was accomplished utilizing additional teams of election observers in the counties included in the study, which enabled the research group to have broader coverage of precincts in each county.

The researchers also added three operational components so that they could better gauge early and Election Day operations and allow more comparability across the observation teams:

- First, each team filled out an observation form for each precinct, and special observation forms were developed specifically for observing polling place opening and closing operations. This allowed for systematic comparability of specific precinct or early voting locations across teams. For example, every observation team had to report on whether voter identification laws were being applied correctly and on the polling place quality. The frequency reports produced from these forms are in the appendix.
- Second, approximately half of the observation team members attended poll worker training so that they would be very knowledgeable about the rules and procedures for opening, closing, and voting. This proved to be very helpful in recognizing additional problems and areas where improvement could be made.
- Third, all the observation teams attended a postelection debriefing so that the researchers could compare experiences across the observation teams regarding areas of strengths and weaknesses, while everyone had these thoughts fresh in his mind.

In 2010, the research team made a number of improvements in preparation for the 2010 study and expanded its scope of reach relative to the 2006 and 2008 study in Bernalillo County. Owing to fewer resources,

the remaining 42% of voters voted on Election Day. See http://www.sos.state.nm.us/08GenResults/Statewide.pdf.

we had to focus our election monitoring efforts on one county. Thus the 2010 observation offers us a different look at how to spread small resources and resource opportunities into useful research. In this case, all the observers were academics or students, both undergraduate and graduate, making them independent of the political parties and candidates. Team members were recruited from two research design courses at the University of New Mexico, one graduate and the other undergraduate. Additionally, advanced graduate students interested in the process were allowed to participate, and one law student who had previously worked with us assisted us again. Graduate students and faculty were paired with undergraduate students to create 16 election-monitoring teams.

Although we had reduced coverage in 2010, only participating in Election Day observations in one county, we had many more teams available to us and had much greater coverage in the Albuquerque metropolitan area. We had a total of 16 teams working two separate shifts, and they observed the voting operations of 269 precincts in 102 locations. The first shift observed from 6:00 A.M. (poll opening) until 1:30 P.M., and the second observed from 1:30 P.M. through closing. We also visited five early voting locations during the early voting period. In addition, we had six team members working as poll workers who reported their Election Day experiences. Thus, even with reduced resources, we were able to professionally observe the 2010 election. Thus a nearby university may be able to assist election administrators in collecting this type of data.

We made appropriate modifications to our 2010 research forms and also added two additional components:

- First, what was mostly voluntary in 2008 with regard to attending training we made mandatory. Every Election Day observer attended poll judge or poll clerk training.
- Second, each team member wrote a one- to three-page Election Day report describing her experiences. These reports provided us with a detailed account and record of each observer's experience and helped us determine consistent problems or particular successes.

We draw from these anecdotes to highlight key problems or experiences of importance. Most of those involved in each iteration of our election monitoring study had considerable previous experience studying and observing elections, not only in New Mexico but also in a variety of other states and nations. However, before the observation effort initiated, all those involved were given briefing materials on the purpose of the study, the details of New Mexico election law, and election observation and monitoring. Observers also participated in a training teleconference as well as other meetings with the observers detailed to each of the four counties.

Working in close consultation with the project principal investigators, each set of observers was assigned to a specific county. Each county team, again working closely with the principal investigators, developed lists of precincts for study. Precincts were chosen for inclusion in the study for a variety of reasons, including geographic location, the type of facility used for the polling place, and to ensure demographic coverage, especially of areas with large Hispanic and predominantly Spanish-speaking populations but also of areas with large Native American populations. Observation teams were provided with credentials, issued by each county, and were also given worksheets for data collection.

Observation teams usually consisted of pairs of project members (in some situations, especially during early voting, observations were done by single individuals). Observer teams that were assigned to Spanish-speaking areas had at least one team member fluent in Spanish.

On Election Day, the observation process had a minimum of three stages and, in some cases, four stages:

- First, observer teams began their work at selected polling places, arriving well before the opening of polls to study the precinct setup process and to complete a special instrument developed specifically for evaluating that process (see the appendix).
- Second, observer teams went to other precincts throughout the day in their respective counties. At each precinct that they studied, they were asked to complete a data collection questionnaire.
- Third, the observer teams stayed in their final precinct at the close of voting, observing and studying the polling place closing procedures. Each team completed a special precinct-closing questionnaire that was developed specifically for evaluating that process.
- Fourth, some observation teams followed the poll workers as they brought their election materials to the collection locations. In some

cases, the observation teams went to the county locations where election materials were collected on election night and where tabulation took place.

Observation team members participated in a debriefing session the day after the election and returned all of their completed questionnaires to the project principal investigators. All data collected were analyzed, and the results of these analyses are reported subsequently (also see Alvarez et al. 2007a; Atkeson et al. 2010b, 2010c, 2011a).

An Important Result: Issues Regarding Voter Identification

In the 2008 study, a key focus of the observation project was how the state's photo identification law was implemented. Therefore the precinct observation instruments were designed to focus on systematic study of this process, and the observation teams were trained to observe this process. In the debriefing and in the subsequent analysis of the structured observation instruments, it became clear that throughout the state, various check-in and voter identification procedures were used. Members of the teams witnessed the following procedures:

1. Voters volunteered identification (pictures or other types of identification cards, especially voter registration cards) without being asked by the poll workers.
2. Voters were told to look up their names in the voter identification roll and provide that number to the poll workers without showing any additional identification.
3. Voters were asked for their names only.
4. Voters were asked for their names and addresses.
5. Voters were asked for their names and birth years.
6. Voters were asked correctly for their names, addresses, and years of birth.
7. Voters were immediately asked for identification, sometimes picture identification, on arrival.
8. Voters were recognized upon entering the polling site and were simply asked to sign the voter rolls.
9. Voters who could not be found in the precinct roll were then asked for identification so that the poll workers could call the

county clerk and request registration status and the correct
voter precinct.

10. Poll workers simply held out their hand with the expectation
that an individual's identification would be placed in it.

Data from the structured observations indicated that poll workers in
about one-quarter of nonrandomly selected precincts that were visited were asking voters for voter identification, and only three in five
(61%) were asking for identification correctly. This confirms survey
data reported by voters and poll workers.

The variation in the check-in procedures and requests for identification are indicative of three issues related to New Mexico polling places
and the way in which the state's voter identification law is structured.
First, the New Mexico voter identification law requires poll workers
to accept multiple forms of identification. All that a voter has to do
to authenticate herself at the polls is to state her name, address, and
birth year. However, a voter can also decide to show a valid form of
photo identification such as a valid driver's license. This encourages
an environment where poll workers can select their preferred form
of identification and request it on check-in. Indeed, in some cases,
observers noted that poll workers altered their procedure depending
on the voter, asking for identification sometimes and not asking for
identification other times.

This variation suggests a second problem, which is that there is a
weakness in poll worker training and a subsequent lack of understanding of the voter identification laws on the part of poll workers. Poll
workers are in a position to make decisions at their polling place, and
when they are not well trained or do not understand a complex law
well, they may choose to implement the law in a way that is easiest for
them, not in a way that reflects the nuanced complexity of the law.

The third factor that leads to greater variability in the way in which
voters are asked to authenticate themselves is a lack of clear signage at
the check-in table. Although in many precincts, there were often "voter
rights signs" and voter identification rules, these were not posted in
places where voters might notice them. In addition, owing to many
precincts being located in schools, the posters simply blended in with
many other colorful posters. In precinct observations in Utah in 2008,
we saw how helpful such signage could be in ensuring that voters

knew how to authenticate themselves, and poll workers did not resort
to choosing their preferred authentication method. Here there was a
placard at the first voting station that said "please state your name
and address," offering a very effective and consistent way to begin
each voter's election experience.

The effects of this confusion and lack of implementation clarity
were obvious to the observers. They reported that when specific forms
of identification were requested and unavailable, sometimes arguments would develop among poll workers over the correct course of
action.

Additionally, there was confusion in some polling locations regarding the proper check-in procedures for individuals who had requested
an absentee ballot. Observers reported that some individuals were
turned away when checking in without their absentee ballots. Additionally, observers reported that some individuals were requested to
go home and search for their absentee ballots and then return after
finding them. In one instance, a team observed a voter being turned
away from the polls because he indicated that he threw the ballot away
and therefore needed a new one to vote. The voter was informed by
the poll worker that if the ballot was thrown away by the voter, a
new ballot could not be issued to him. Under some interpretations
of New Mexico election law, the voter could have cast a provisional
ballot.

Findings and Recommendations: Linking Evaluations and Action

In this and the previous chapters, we have discussed how election auditing and performance-based management should provide performance-
based management information that can be acted on by the election
official and the elections office and can inform policy makers more
generally. The idea behind creating a set of policy recommendations
from the auditing and performance-based management is to create specific, actionable recommendations for how to improve the problems
identified. The multifaceted evaluation process we have proposed in
this book allows these recommendations to be made based on data
from different sources and based on different experiences – those
of voters, poll workers, and outside observers – within the election
process.

These results, along with those from our voter and poll worker data, led our research group to issue a number of recommendations regarding voter identification issues in New Mexico:

Recommendation 1: Poll worker training should emphasize the importance of uniformity in election rules and administration across precincts. This is especially true for voter identification procedures, which should be followed even in small communities where poll workers may be familiar with many voters.

Recommendation 2: Prior to the opening of the polls, all poll workers should be required to read the voter identification law to ensure that all workers understand the law and to ensure consistency among poll workers.

Recommendation 3: There should be a sign placed at the first station on the check-in table. This sign could be a two-sided placard placed on the registration desk so that both the worker and voter may read the sign at check-in. The sign would reflect a uniform standard procedure for beginning the check-in process: "voter should state their name, address, and year of birth." If a voter cannot meet the standard procedure, then a backup form of identification (photo identification) may be requested.

Recommendation 4: Election Day precincts may want to adopt the method we observed in early voting, where voters provided their names, addresses, and birth years on a piece of paper and then presented that information to the poll worker for voter authentication.

Recommendation 5: New Mexico law allows a voter to vote provisionally at her precinct if she had requested an absentee ballot (Section 1–12–8). If a ballot is destroyed in any way, even if by the voter herself, a voter should be allowed to obtain a new ballot and vote provisionally. This facet of law should also be stressed more in poll worker training.

Designing an Effective Election Observation Study

As is evident from the extensive presentation of the multiyear New Mexican election observation effort, a great deal can be learned about election administration practices with boots on the ground. Observers have a chance to see exactly how procedures are implemented on the ground, they have a fantastic opportunity to see how procedural implementations vary between polling locations, and they have an opportunity to interact with polling place workers and, on occasion, voters themselves.

On the basis of our experiences with observation efforts, we think there are a number of important lessons and recommendations that can help others have effective observation studies designed for election performance analyses.

First, *context is key*. For observers to be efficient and effective, they need to understand the procedural, political, and legal contexts of the jurisdiction. We learned this important lesson as we observed elections in New Mexico in 2006 and then again in 2008. In 2006, we found a number of Election Day voting issues, including issues with electioneering, voter privacy, and inconsistent applications of voter identification procedures. Those observations gave us an important framework for our 2008 efforts, as we were able to frame specific research hypotheses about the sorts of issues that we anticipated would arise in that election. Importantly, we were able to continue this process in 2010.

Second, *consistency is important*. A potential issue with participant observation methods is that the observers might have inconsistent methods for their observation effort, they might collect information in different ways, or their evaluations themselves may be heterogeneous. There are a number of ways that observation efforts can be made more consistent: preobservation training; matching experienced observers with less experienced observers, as in 2010; and the provision of well-designed, uniform data collection forms. All of these are important to ensure that the information received from election observation efforts is as consistent as possible.

Third, *coverage is critical*. It is critical that observation efforts be both geographically and procedurally extensive. One of the amazing things about elections is how heterogeneous the local administration can be: in the same jurisdiction, on the same Election Day, one is likely to see voting in very different physical locations (churches, schools, government buildings, fire stations, residences), in very different parts of a jurisdiction (ranging from highly urban areas to highly rural areas), in very different demographic areas (racially and based on income distributions) with different political contexts. Any election observation effort needs to take as much of this heterogeneity into consideration as possible. In addition, we see that, increasingly, elections are also administered in diverse ways. For example, in most states, elections are now a complex procedural mixture of in-person early voting, voting by mail, and voting in person on Election Day. Capturing this heterogeneity is also critical for any observational effort because the voting experiences and procedural issues can be vastly different across these different methods of voting.

Finally, *credibility is necessary*. For an election observation effort to work, the observers and their research efforts need to be credible. The observers need the trust of the election administrators, poll workers, and other stakeholders in the process. Election observers need access to all aspects of an election administration process to study it in detail, and for that access, they need to work with (not against) election officials and stakeholders. Election observers need the trust of poll workers and stakeholders so that they know that the observers are there only to observe and study.

Conclusion

It has been more than a decade since the events in the 2000 presidential election, especially in Florida, focused attention on voting technologies and election administration in the United States. During that time, researchers have made great strides working to understand what works, and what does not, in how elections are run in the United States and across the world. It is easy to forget that in the aftermath of the 2000 election, the book on election administration that was most current was a text written by Joseph Harris in 1934. Political scientists had clearly studied issues such as the effects of voter registration on turnout and residual votes (ballot roll-off in down ballot races), but the idea of studying elections for the purpose of improving the mechanics of our democracy and improving administration and implementation was not something on which many people were focused.[1]

Over the past decade, researchers have generated many reports, articles, and books on election administration and voting technology.

---

[1] We would like to single out one scholar – Robert Montjoy, a professor of political science at the University of New Orleans – as an exception to this. Montjoy has been working with election officials for a long time and had been expressing concerns about the quality of elections for a while prior to the 2000 election. He was one of the creators of the Certified Election/Registration Administrator program at Auburn University. Unfortunately, before the 2000 election, there was little interest in either public administration or political science in studying election administration – something that public administration scholars often view as being "too political science" and political scientists often view as being "too public administration."

However, although much of this research has been quite valuable, it has not been accompanied by the development of a set of tools that can easily be applied to evaluate the performance of or effectiveness of election administration, either in a particular area (e.g., voter registration) or across the entirety of an election. This book has discussed a variety of evaluative tools, applied them to different electoral contexts, and discussed different examples of how these tools can be used to effectively gauge whether elections are well run in a particular place.

The measures and methods we have presented here have been applied in certain election jurisdictions, with the best example being New Mexico. There we had the opportunity to work closely and repeatedly with election officials to use these tools in recent elections to understand where the state's election reform efforts had succeeded and where they had fallen short. This allowed us to provide valuable information to policy makers and election officials regarding the places that needed improvement and the places that were highly successful. The election officials in New Mexico continue to use tools that we have discussed here – and other election officials in jurisdictions like Los Angeles and Washington, D.C., have begun to use these same tools. The adoption of these efforts in various jurisdictions demonstrates to us that there is a pressing need for a more widespread initiative to document the effectiveness of election administration across the nation.

Calls to improve the collection of data about election administration are not new. For example, in 2001, the Caltech/MIT Voting Technology Project (VTP; 2001a, 76) argued, "The conduct of elections would be significantly improved in the United States if the amount of locally produced information about election administration were more broadly and systematically collected and reported to the public, to the press, and to election administrators nationwide." The VTP went on to discuss a variety of the sort of relatively straightforward measures that we have also mentioned in this book. For example, there should be quality data reported, after every election, regarding the voting technologies used for in-person and early voting, any problems that arose with registration, the rejection rate of absentee ballots and the reason for rejection, the results of comprehensive or postelection auditing, the rate of use of provisional ballots as well the rate of rejection of such ballots and the reason for rejection, and the costs of election administration.

It's important to note that the U.S. Election Assistance Commission (EAC) was formed as a result of the Help America Vote Act (HAVA) and that one of its primary functions in recent years has been collecting and distributing this information after each federal election. However, the EAC was not given the power to require state or local governments to provide any of these data to the EAC, nor has the EAC been given the funds to create a data collection system that would facilitate such data collection. As Thad Hall and Dan Tojaki have argued, one solution to the data collection problem would be for the federal government to pay states for it.[2] They argued that the federal government and the states would engage in a trade:

> The federal government would provide an ongoing source of funds for state and local governments to run elections. In return, state and local officials would have the obligation to collect and provide to the federal government data on the performance of their election systems. States that provide quality precinct-level data get paid. Those that provide incomplete or inaccurate data would not get paid.

Such a system would provide useful data that could be used for performance-based management and for assessments of elections by scholars and policy makers.

Regardless of how we get there, as we have noted in this book, we can and should do better. Elections are a vital aspect of our democracy, and the individuals who have a great deal at stake in elections (candidates) are often later in a position to have an important influence on election officials once they are in office. Not surprisingly, the importance of elections makes election officials risk averse; an error in implementing a new electoral change can change the outcome of an election, which can affect who comes into office and the policy direction of a local, a state, or the federal government. However, this does not mean that election officials should be afraid to measure their performance.

Better measurement and evaluation of election administration will require an important cultural change in how the public views elections, how policy makers regulate elections, and how election administrators view their role. In our experience, election officials typically are well

[2] http://moritzlaw.osu.edu/blogs/tokaji/2007_06_01_equalvote_archive.html.

meaning and are often (deservedly) proud of the hard work that they and their staff put into each election. However, election officials need to be willing to take on the political risks associated with collecting performance-based metrics. These data will allow them to improve their election management and also better communicate with voters, stakeholders, and candidates about what is working and what needs to be improved in the election process.

At the same time, policy makers need to be willing to change antiquated laws and regulations that stymie the efforts of states to collect the data they need or to manage their elections effectively. For example, the state of Georgia requires its elections to be certified in less than three days because of the state's runoff election law. This time is very short – too short for local election officials to do their jobs effectively and audit the work that is being done. Likewise, states that do not require that local election officials report the number of voters who voted, or that do not count absentee, early, and Election Day ballots separately, so that problems with any of these vote modes can be identified, limit the ability of performance-based election management. State and local governments also have to be willing to fund elections appropriately, especially the training of poll workers. Finally, state and local governments have to recognize that they often put extraordinary demands on election officials when they make numerous changes to election laws at the same time. In Washington, D.C., in 2010, the government was asked to implement several major reforms all at once – without appropriate increases in staffing and funding – which put an incredible strain on election officials and their staff.

We hope that we have documented in this book the utility of performance-based evaluation for election administration and that many election officials will be convinced that these tools will allow them to work to improve their election processes. However, we also hope that policy makers will see the utility in performance-based evaluation and that they will develop an appropriate policy framework so that these metrics can be used to determine how well elections are run in their states or localities and throughout the nation. Such a framework will require providing resources to election officials and researchers to collect and analyze the sorts of metrics that we have discussed in this book. This framework will require policy makers to develop a process for rewarding election jurisdictions that are doing

150

Evaluating Elections

well and mechanisms for providing resources to improve elections in those jurisdictions that are not performing well. Only when we have the resources in place to produce performance evaluations – and to use those studies to provide better elections – will we begin to resolve many of the problems that continue to plague elections in the United States.

There are many ways in which a performance-based evaluation process might work. For example, HAVA required that states develop a process to quickly assess their needs and to develop a State Plan – a document spelling out each state's vision for how it would use the funding provided by HAVA to improve its election administration process. A similar model could be developed in each state, where local jurisdictions could develop performance-based evaluation plans and then obtain funding to put their performance-based evaluation process into operation. The data and evaluation reports could then be made available to stakeholders and the public, and the results of the evaluation would then be used to allocate funds to improve election administration in future elections. Those investments would be assessed by future evaluation studies, and the process would continue. We would then be in a situation where election administrators had a process that would facilitate improvement of election performance; there would be much more information and data available to the public and stakeholders that would likely make them more confident in the process; and the availability of the evaluation data would help drive new research that would result in additional improvements in the study and administration of elections in the future.

Appendix: Precinct Opening, Closing, Election Day Forms

Election Day Open Polls Observation Worksheet
2008 Presidential Election, November 4, 2008 – New Mexico
(This Form Is for Opening Polls Only!)

In addition to this form, please fill out a general observation form for this precinct.

Please fill out a form for each individual precinct, even if there are multiple precincts at a single location. When appropriate, ask poll workers, poll judges, or observers for their observations for answers to questions that took place during periods when you were not present or events that are taking place currently. When a situation is different than it should be, please elaborate as much as possible. Always feel free to add notes and other observations. Please write as much as you like about each precinct.

Polling Location Information

Polling Location Name and Number:_____

Type of Polling Location (church, school, etc.)_____

Other Precinct Number(s) at Location:_____

City:_____ County:_____

Names of Observers:_____

Time of Arrival:_____ AM/PM Time of Departure:_____ AM/PM

1a. Did the presiding judge show up at the precinct on time?
    Yes   No

1b. Did all the poll workers show up on time? (Please explain any tardiness issues in the comments section of this form)
    Yes   No

2. Did poll workers check to make sure the yellow warehouse slip numbers match the M100?
    Yes   No

3. Did they verify the ballot bins in the M100 are empty?
    Yes   No

4. Was the zero-tape generated?
    Yes   No

5. Was the zero-tape signed by all the poll workers?
    Yes   No

6. Was the zero-tape left on the machine or was it detached?
    Yes   No

7. Was the signature voter roster signed by all the poll workers?
    Yes   No

8. Was the checklist voter roster signed by all the poll workers?
    Yes   No

9. Was the registered voter list posted at the precinct and easily visible?
    Yes   No

10. Was the voter bill of rights posted at the precinct and easily visible?
    Yes   No

11. Were sample ballots posted at the precinct and easily visible?
    Yes   No

12. Was the ballot marking example sign posted at the precinct and easily visible?
    Yes   No

13. Was the voter identification poster posted at the precinct and easily visible?
    Yes   No

14. Additional Comments:

Election Day Polling General Observation Worksheet
2008 Presidential Election, November 4, 2008 – New Mexico

Please fill out a form for each individual precinct, even if there are multiple precincts at a single location. When appropriate, ask poll workers, poll judges, or observers for their observations for answers to questions that took place during periods when you were not present or events that are taking place currently. When a situation is different than it should be, please elaborate as much as possible. Always feel free to add notes and other observations. Please write as much as you like about each precinct.

Polling Location Information
Polling Location Name and Number:_____
Type of Polling Location (church, school, etc.)_____
Other Precinct Number(s) at Location:_____
City: _____ County:_____
Names of Observers:_____
Time of Arrival:_____ AM/PM Time of Departure:_____ AM/PM
----

1. Was the voting location easy to find and clearly marked?
   Yes   No
2. Was the accessibility to the voting location easy for voters (esp. handicapped)?
   Yes   No
3. Was there only one entrance into the voting location?
   Yes   No
4. Was there adequate parking at the polling location?
   Yes   No
5. Were all campaign materials located at least 100 feet from the polling location?
   Yes   No
6. Were there people holding political signs outside the polling location?
   Yes   No
7. How many poll workers were working at the time you were present?

8a. Was there a line of voters?

Yes   No

8b. If there was a line, were voters waiting to checkin or waiting to vote?

Checkin   Vote

8c. Estimate the amount of time a voter waited to vote:

9. Was it noisy inside the polling location?

Yes   No

10. Was it crowded inside the polling location?

Yes   No

11a. Were there party observers present at this polling location?

Yes   No

11b. If so, from which political parties?

12. Were there lawyers present at this location to help poll workers?

Yes   No

13. Were poll workers asking voters for voter identification (such as a photo ID)?

Yes   No

14a. Based on your observations, were they asking for identification appropriately?

Yes   No

14b. If no, please explain:

15. Were poll workers checking voter names on two lists?

Yes   No

16. Did you see poll workers handing out voter registration forms to anyone?

Yes   No

17. Can you estimate the ages of the poll workers at this location?

18a. Was at least one of the poll workers bilingual?

Yes   No

18b. Did you see the poll workers help someone in a language other than English?

Yes   No

19. Were no cell phone signs posted?

Yes   No

20. Did you see anyone using a cell phone in the voting booth or at the voting location?

 Yes No

21. Did voters have adequate privacy while filling out their ballots?

 Yes No

22. Did you see anyone voting outside of a privacy booth?

 Yes No

23. Was the Automark set up, operational, and available for use?

 Yes No

24. Did you observe anybody use the Automark?

 Yes No

25a. Were there any reported problems with the M100 voting tabulators?

 Yes No

25b. If yes, please explain:

26. Were the keys removed from the M100s?

 Yes No

27. Where were the unused **Paper Ballots** being stored?

28. Where and how were the completed **Provisional Ballots** stored?

29. Where and how were the completed **In Lieu Of Ballots** stored?

30. Did you see any voters bring their absentee ballots to the precinct?

 Yes No

31. Where and how were the dropped off absentee ballots stored?

32. Did unused ballots appear to be secure from the public?

 Yes No

33a. Did anyone but the voter handle a spoiled ballot?

 Yes No

33b. If yes, please explain how the spoiled ballot was handled:

34. Were voters who spoiled ballots allowed to take the spoiled ballot with them to vote a new ballot?

 Yes No

35. Where and how were the **Spoiled Ballots** stored?

36a. Were ballots being fed into the M100s by voters or poll workers?

 Voters Poll Workers Both

36b. If they were being fed by poll workers, were the poll workers taking them from all voters, or only voters who asked for help?

All Voters   Only Voters Who Asked for Help

37. Were the poll workers collecting permit cards from voters as they fed their ballot into the M100?

Yes   No

38. How were the voter permit cards stored after being returned to poll workers?

39. Additional Comments:

Election Day Close Polls Observation Worksheet
2008 Presidential Election, November 4, 2008 – New Mexico
(This Form Is for Closing Polls Only!)

In addition to this form, please fill out a general observation form for this precinct.

Please fill out a form for each individual precinct, even if there are multiple precincts at a single location. When appropriate, ask poll workers, poll judges, or observers for their observations for answers to questions that took place during periods when you were not present or events that are taking place currently. When a situation is different than it should be, please elaborate as much as possible. Always feel free to add notes and other observations. Please write as much as you like about each precinct.

Polling Location Information
Polling Location Name and Number:_____
Type of Polling Location (church, school, etc.)_____
Other Precinct Number(s) at Location:_____
City: _____ County:_____
Names of Observers:_____
Time of Arrival:_____ AM/PM Time of Departure:_____ AM/PM
----

1. Were there any voters still in line waiting to vote when the polls closed?

Yes   No

2. Did the poll workers balance the number of voters, the public count, with the M100 tape?

   Yes   No

3a. Was there a problem balancing the # of voters with the # of ballots cast at closing?

   Yes   No

3b. If yes, how was the problem resolved?

4. Did the poll workers post a copy of the election results at the location for the public to view?

   Yes   No

5. Did poll workers place the ballots in the ballot box?

   Yes   No

6. Were spoiled ballots also included in the ballot box?

   Yes   No

7. Was the ballot box padlocked?

   Yes   No

8. Were the 2 sets of keys for the locked ballot box placed in different envelopes?

   Yes   No

9. Did the poll workers destroy all the unused ballots?

   Yes   No

10. Were the stubs of unused ballots removed prior to destroying them?

   Yes   No

11. What did the poll workers do with the stubs of unused ballots?

12a. Was anything other than ballots placed in the ballot box?

   Yes   No

12b. If yes, please describe what those items were:

13. Did you see poll workers attempt to feed any uncounted ballots (placed in the emergency slot in the M100) into the M100 after polls closed?

   Yes   No

14a. Did they have to hand tally any ballots?

   Yes   No

14b. If yes, about how long did this take?

14c. How many poll workers were involved in hand tallying?

15. How were provisional and in lieu of ballots separated and orga-
    nized?
16a. Did the poll workers use any chain of custody forms?
    Yes   No
16b. If yes, for what purposes?
17. Was the PCMCIA card removed from the M100?
    Yes   No
18. Additional Comments (please also describe the drop-off pro-
    cess):

References

Abbink, Jon, and Wim Van Binsbergen. 2000. "International Election Observation: A Discussion on Policy and Practice." In *Election Observation and Democratization in Africa*, ed. Gerti Hasseling and Jon Abbink. New York: Palgrave Macmillan.

Alvarez, R. Michael, and Thad E. Hall. 2004. *Point, Click, and Vote*. Washington, DC: Brookings Institution Press.

Alvarez, R. Michael, and Thad E. Hall. 2006. "Controlling Democracy: The Principal-Agent Problems in Election Administration." *Policy Studies Journal*, 34(4): 491–510.

Alvarez, R. Michael, and Thad E. Hall. 2008a. "Building Secure and Transparent Elections through Standard Operating Procedures." *Public Administration Review*, 68: 827–837.

Alvarez, R. Michael, and Thad E. Hall. 2008b. *Electronic Elections: The Perils and Promises of Digital Democracy*. Princeton, NJ: Princeton University Press.

Alvarez, R. Michael, and Thad E. Hall. 2009. "Provisional Ballots in the 2008 Ohio General Election," Pew Charitable Trusts, The Center for the States, *Provisional Ballots: An Imperfect Solution*, at: http://www.pewcenteronthestates.org/initiatives_detail.aspx?initiativeID=54789.

Alvarez, R. Michael, Stephen Ansolabehere, and Charles Stewart III. 2005. "Studying Elections: Data Quality and Pitfalls in Measuring of Effects of Voting Technologies." *Policy Studies Journal*, 33(1): 15–24.

Alvarez, R. Michael, Lonna Atkeson, and Thad Hall. 2007a. "The New Mexico Election Administration Report: The 2006 New Mexico Election." http://vote2006.unm.edu/.

Alvarez, R. Michael, Thad E. Hall, and Morgan H. Llewellyn. 2007b. "How Hard Can It Be: Do Citizens Think It Is Difficult to Register to Vote?" *Stanford Law and Policy Review*, 18(349): 382–409.

Alvarez, R. Michael, Thad E. Hall, and Susan D. Hyde, eds. 2008a. *Election Fraud: Detecting and Deterring Electoral Manipulation.*Washington, DC: Brookings Institution Press.

Alvarez, R. Michael, Thad E. Hall, and Morgan H. Llewellyn. 2008b. "Are Americans Confident Their Ballots Are Counted?" *Journal of Politics*, 70(2): 754–766.

Alvarez, R. Michael, Thad E. Hall, and Betsy Sinclair. 2008c. "Whose Absentee Votes Are Returned and Counted: The Variety and Use of Absentee Ballots in California." *Electoral Studies*, 27(4): 673–683.

Alvarez, R. Michael, Stephen Ansolabehere, Adam Berinsky, Gabriel Lenz, Charles Stewart III, and Thad E. Hall. 2009a. *2008 Survey of the Performance of American Elections*. Boston, MA/Pasadena, CA: Caltech/MIT Voting Technology Project.

Alvarez, R. Michael, Thad E. Hall, and Morgan H. Llewellyn. 2009b. "The Winner's Effect: Voter Confidence before and after the 2006 Elections." Working Paper. http://vote.caltech.edu/.

Alvarez, R. Michael, Jeff Jonas, William E. Winkler, and Rebecca N. Wright. 2009c. "Interstate Voter Registration Database Matching: The Oregon – Washington 2008 Pilot Project." Paper presented at the 2009 Electronic Voting Technology Workshop/Workshop on Trustworthy Elections, Montreal, Canada.

Alvarez, R. Michael, Charles Stewart III, and Thad E. Hall. 2010. "Voting Technology and the Election Experience: The 2009 Gubernatorial Races in New Jersey and Virginia." In *Electronic Voting 2010*, ed. Robert Krimmer and Rüdiger Grimm. Bonn, Germany: Gesellschaft für Informatik.

Alvarez, R. Michael, Dustin Beckett, and Charles Stewart III. 2011. "Voting Technology, Vote-by-Mail, and Residual Votes in California, 1990–2010." Voting Technology Project Working Paper 105. http://ssrn.com/abstract= 1837946.

Alvarez, R. Michael, Lonna Rae Atkeson, and Thad E. Hall, eds. 2012. *Confirming Elections: Creating Confidence and Integrity through Election Auditing*. New York: Palgrave.

Alvarez, R. Michael, Lonna Rae Atkeson, Thad E. Hall, and Jessica Taverna. 2012. "Confirming Elections: Creating Confidence and Integrity through Election Auditing." In *Confirming Elections: Creating Confidence and Integrity through Election Auditing*, ed. Thad E. Hall, Lonna Rae Atkeson, and R. Michael Alvarez. New York: Palgrave.

Ansolabehere, Stephen. 2002. "Voting Machines, Race and Equal Protection." *Election Law Journal*, 1(1): 61–70.

Ansolabehere, Stephen. 2007. "Election Administration and Voting Rights Renewal of the Voting Rights Act." In *The Future of the Voting Rights Act*, ed. David Epstein, Richard Pildes, Rudolfo de la Garza, and Sharyn O'Hallaran. New York: Russell Sage Foundation.

Ansolabehere, Stephen. 2008a. "Access versus Integrity in Voter Identification Requirements." *New York University Annual Survey of American Law*, 63(4): 613–630.

Ansolabehere, Stephen. 2008b. "Voting Technology and Election Law." In *America Votes! A Guide to Modern Election Law and Voting Rights*, ed. Benjamin Griffith. Washington, DC: American Bar Association.

Ansolabehere, Stephen, and Charles Stewart III. 2005. "Residual Votes Attributable to Technology." *Journal of Politics*, 67(2): 365–389.

Ansolabehere, Stephen, and Andrew Reeves. 2012. "Using Recounts to Measure the Accuracy of Vote Tabulations: Evidence from New Hampshire Elections 1946–2002." In *Confirming Elections: Creating Confidence and Integrity through Election Auditing*, ed. Thad E. Hall, Lonna Rae Atkeson, and R. Michael Alvarez. New York: Palgrave.

Ansolabehere, Stephen, Eitan Hersh, Alan Gerber, and David Doherty. 2010. "Voter Registration List Quality Pilot Studies: A Report on Methodology." Unpublished manuscript.

Atkeson, Lonna Rae. 2007a. "The 2006 New Mexico Election Administration Voter Report." University of New Mexico.

Atkeson, Lonna Rae. 2007b. "The 2006 Colorado Election Administration Voter Report." University of New Mexico.

Atkeson, Lonna Rae, and Kyle L. Saunders. 2007. "Voter Confidence: A Local Matter?" *PS: Political Science and Politics*, 40: 655–660.

Atkeson, Lonna Rae, and Lori Tafoya. 2008. "Surveying Political Activists: An Examination of the Effectiveness of a Mixed Mode (Internet and Mail) Survey Design." *Journal of Elections, Public Opinion, and Parties*, 18(4): 367–386.

Atkeson, Lonna Rae, and Alex N. Adams. 2010. "Mixed Mode (Internet and Mail) Probability Samples and Survey Representativeness: The Case of New Mexico 2008." Paper presented at the Western Political Science Association, San Francisco, CA.

Atkeson, Lonna Rae, R. Michael Alvarez, Thad E. Hall, Lisa A. Bryant, Yann Kereval, Morgan Llewellyn, and David Odegaard. 2008a. "The 2008 New Mexico Post Election Audit Report." University of New Mexico.

Atkeson, Lonna Rae, R. Michael Alvarez, and Thad E. Hall. 2008b. "The New Mexico 2006 Post Election Audit Report." http://www.unm.edu/~atkeson/documents/NM_Audit_Report.pdf.

Atkeson, Lonna Rae, R. Michael Alvarez, Thad E. Hall. 2009. "Provisional Voting in New Mexico," Pew Charitable Trusts, The Center for the States, *Provisional Ballots: An Imperfect Solution*, at: http://www.pewcenteronthestates.org/initiatives_detail.aspx?initiativeID=54789.

Atkeson, Lonna Rae, Alex N. Adams, and R. Michael Alvarez. 2010a. "Assessing Data Quality across Probability Samples: An Examination of a Post General Election Mixed-Mode (Internet and Mail) and Telephone Survey."

Paper presented at the American Association of Public Opinion Research, Chicago, IL.

Atkeson, Lonna Rae, Alex N. Adams, Lisa Bryant, Angelina Gonzalez-Aller, Willard Hunter, Yann Kerevel, Kimberly Proctor, Lisa Sanchez, and Lori Tafoya. 2010b. "The City of Albuquerque 2009 Mayoral Election Administration Report." University of New Mexico.

Atkeson, Lonna Rae, R. Michael Alvarez, and Thad E. Hall. 2010c. "Assessing Electoral Performance in New Mexico Using an Eco-system Approach: New Mexico 2008." University of New Mexico. http://www.unm.edu/~atkeson/newmexico.html.

Atkeson, Lonna Rae, R. Michael Alvarez, and Thad E. Hall. 2010d. "The New Mexico Pilot Project." In *Confirming Elections: Creating Confidence and Integrity through Election Auditing*, ed. Thad E. Hall, Lonna Rae Atkeson, and R. Michael Alvarez. New York: Palgrave.

Atkeson, Lonna Rae, Lisa Bryant, Thad Hall, Kyle L Saunders, and R. Michael Alvarez. 2010e. "New Barriers to Voter Participation: An Examination of New Mexico's Voter Identification Law." *Electoral Studies*, 29(1): 66–73.

Atkeson, Lonna Rae. R. Michael Alvarez. Alex N. Adams, and Lisa Bryant. 2011a. "The 2010 New Mexico Election Administration Report. Typescript, University of New Mexico. Available at: http://www.unm.edu/~atkeson/newmexico.html.

Atkeson, Lonna Rae, Lisa A. Bryant, Alex N. Adams, Luciana Zilberman, and Kyle L. Saunders, 2011b. "Considering Mixed Mode Surveys for Questions in Political Behavior: Using the Internet and Mail to Get Quality Data at Reasonable Costs." *Political Behavior*, 33: 161–178.

Atkeson, Lonna Rae, R. Michael Alvarez, and Thad E. Hall. 2012. "The New Mexico Pilot Project." In *Confirming Elections: Creating Confidence and Integrity through Election Auditing*, ed. Thad E. Hall, Lonna Rae Atkeson, and R. Michael Alvarez. New York: Palgrave.

Atkeson, Lonna Rae, Yann Kerevel, R. Michael Alvarez, and Thad E. Hall. 2012. "Who Asks for Voter Identification?" Typescript, University of New Mexico.

Bjornlund, Eric. 2004. *Beyond Free and Fair: Monitoring Elections and Building Democracy*. Washington, DC: Woodrow Wilson Press.

Blumberg, Stephen J., and Julian V. Luke. 2011. "Wireless Substitution: Early Release of Estimates from the National Health Interview Survey, January–June 2011." http://www.cdc.gov/nchs/data/nhis/earlyrelease/wireless201112.htm.

Bouckaert, Geert, and B. Guy Peters. 2002. "Performance Measurement and Management: The Achilles' Heel in Administrative Modernization." *Public Performance and Management Review*, 25(4): 359–362.

Brady, Henry E., Justin Buchler, Matt Jarvis, and John McNulty. 2001a. "Counting All the Votes: The Performance of Voting Technology in the

United States." Report published by the Survey Research Center and Institute of Governmental Studies, University of California, Berkeley.

Brady, Henry E., Michael C. Herron, Walter R. Mebane Jr., Jasjeet Singh Sekhon, Kenneth W. Shotts, and Jonathan Wand. 2001b. "Law and Data: The Butterfly Ballot Episode." *PS: Political Science and Politics,* 34(1): 59–69.

Brown, Stephen. 2005. "Foreign Aid and Democracy Promotion: Lessons from Africa." *European Journal of Development Research,* 17(2): 179–198.

Bryant, Lisa A. 2010. "Voter Confidence and the Use of Absentee Ballots and Electronic Voting Equipment: An Experimental Study." Paper presented at the American Political Science Association Annual Meeting, Washington, DC.

Buchler, Justin, Matthew Jarvis, and John E. McNulty. 2004. "Punch Card Technology and the Racial Gap in Residual Votes." *Perspective on Politics,* 2(3): 517–524.

Bullock, Charles S., III, M. V. Hood III, and Richard Clark. 2005. "Punchcards, Jim Crow, and Al Gore: Explaining Voter Trust in the Electoral System in Georgia, 2000." *State Politics and Policy Quarterly,* 5(3): 283–294.

Byrne, Michael D., Kristen K. Greene, and Sarah P. Everett. 2007. "Usability of Voting Systems: Baseline Data for Paper, Punch Cards, and Lever Machines." Paper presented at the SIGCHI Conference on Human Factors in Computing Systems, San Jose, CA.

Bryant, Lisa A. 2010. "Voter Confidence and the Use of Absentee Ballots and Electronic Voting Equipment: An Experimental Study." Paper presented at the American Political Science Association Annual Meeting, Washington, DC.

Caltech/MIT Voting Technology Project. 2001a. "Voting: What Is, What Could Be." http://vote.caltech.edu/.

Caltech/MIT Voting Technology Project. 2001b. "Residual Votes Attributable to Technology: An Assessment of the Reliability of Existing Voting Equipment." http://www.hss.caltech.edu/~voting/CalTech_MIT_Report_Version2.pdf.

Card, David, and Enrico Moretti. 2007. "Does Voting Technology Affect Election Outcomes? Touch-Screen Voting and the 2004 Presidential Elections." *Review of Economics and Statistics,* 89(4): 660–673.

Carothers, Thomas. 1997. "The Observers Observed." *Journal of Democracy,* 8(3): 17–31.

Century Foundation. 2004. "Voting in 2004: A Report to the Nation on America's Election Process." http://tcf.org/events/2004/ev132.

Cobb, Rachael V., D. James Greiner, and Kevin M. Quinn. 2012. "Can Voter ID Laws Be Administered in a Race-Neutral Manner? Evidence from the City of Boston in 2008." *Quarterly Journal of Political Science.*

Commission on Federal Election Reform. 2005. "Building Confidence in U.S. Elections." Center for Democracy and Elections Management, American University.

Dee, Thomas S. 2007. "Technology and Voter Intent: Evidence from the California Recall Election." *Review of Economics and Statistics*, 89(4): 674–683.

Delli Carpini, Michael X., and Scott Keeter. 1997.*What Americans Know about Politics and Why It Matters*. New Haven, CT: Yale University Press.

Dillman, Don A. 2000. *Mail and Internet Surveys: The Tailored Design Method*. 2nd ed. New York: John Wiley.

Dillman, Don A., Jolene D. Smyth, and Leah Melani Christian. 2009. *Internet, Mail, and Mixed-Mode Surveys: The Tailored Design Method*. 3rd ed. Hoboken, NJ: John Wiley.

Dilulio, John J., Gerald Garvey, and Donald F. Kettl. 1993. *Improving Government Performance: An Owner's Manual*. Washington, DC: Brookings Institution Press.

Downs, Anthony. 1957. *An Economic Theory of Democracy*. New York: Harper and Brothers.

Elklit, Jørgen, and Andrew Reynolds. 2005. "A Framework for the Systematic Study of Election Quality." *Democratization*, 12(2): 147–162.

Everett, Sarah P., Michael D. Byrne, and Kristen K. Greene. 2006. "Measuring the Usability of Paper Ballots: Efficiency, Effectiveness, and Satisfaction." Paper presented at the Human Factors and Ergonomics Society 50th Annual Meeting, San Francisco, CA.

Federal Election Commission. (n.d.). *The Impact of the National Voter Registration Act of 1993 on the Administration of Elections for Federal Office 1999–2000*. http://www.eac.gov/assets/1/AssetManager/The%20Impact%20of%20the%20National%20Voter%20Registration%20Act%20on%20Federal%20Elections%201999-2000.pdf.

Frisina, Laurin, Michael C. Herron, James Honaker, and Jeffrey B. Lewis. 2008. "Ballot Formats, Touchscreens, and Undervotes: A Study of the 2006 Midterm Elections in Florida." *Election Law Journal*, 7(1): 25–47.

Geisler, Gisela. 1993. "Fair? What Has Fairness Got to Do with It? Vagaries of Election Observations and Democratic Standards." *Journal of Modern African Studies*, 31(4): 613–637.

Gerken, Heather K. 2009. *The Democracy Index: Why Our Election System Is Failing and How to Fix It*. Princeton, NJ: Princeton University Press.

Gomez, Brad T., Thomas G. Hansford and George A. Krause. 2007. "The Republicans Should Pray for Rain: Weather, Turnout, and Voting in U.S. Presidential Elections" *Journal of Politics* 69 (August): 649–663.

Green, Donald P. and Alan S. Gerber. 2008. *Get Out the Vote: How to Increase Voter Turnout*. Washington, D.C.: Brookings Institution Press.

Groves, Robert M. 2004. *Survey Errors and Survey Costs*. Hoboken, NJ: Wiley-Interscience.

Hall, Thad E. 2003. "Public Participation in Election Management: The Case of Language Minority Voters." *American Review of Public Administration*, 33(4): 407–422.

Hall, Thad E., and Epp Maaten. 2008. "Improving the Transparency of Remote E-Voting: The Estonian Experience." In *Electronic Voting 2008*, ed. Robert Krimmer and Rüdiger Grimm. Bonn, Germany: Gesellschaft für Informatik.

Hall, Thad E., and Charles Stewart III. 2011. "Voter Attitudes toward Poll Workers in the 2008 Election." Caltech/MIT Voting Technology Project.

Hall, Thad E., and Tova Wang. 2008. "Normative Principles for Evaluating Election Fraud." In *Election Fraud: Detecting and Preventing Electoral Manipulation*, ed. Michael Alvarez, Thad Hall, and Susan Hyde. Washington, DC: Brookings Institution Press.

Hall, Thad E., J. Quin Monson, and Kelly Patterson. 2007. "Poll Workers in American Democracy: An Early Assessment." *P.S.: Political Science and Politics.* 40 (4): 647–654.

Hall, Thad E., J. Quin Monson, and Kelly Patterson. 2008. "Poll Workers and American Democracy." In *Democracy in the States: Experiments in Election Reform*, ed. Bruce Cain, Todd Donovan, and Caroline Tolbert. Washington, DC: Brookings Institution Press.

Hall, Thad E., J. Quin Monson, and Kelly Patterson. 2009. "The Human Dimension of Elections: How Poll Workers Shape Public Confidence in Elections." *Political Research Quarterly*, 62(3): 507–522.

Hanmer, Michael J., Won-Ho Park, Michael W. Traugott, Richard G. Niemi, Paul S. Herrnson, Benjamin B. Bederson, and Frederick C. Conrad. 2010. "Losing Fewer Votes: The Impact of Changing Voting Systems on Residual Votes." *Political Research Quarterly*, 63: 129–142.

Hatry, Harry. 1999. *Performance Measurement: Getting Results.* 2nd ed. Washington, DC: Urban Institute Press.

Heidelbaugh, Heather S., Logan S. Fisher, and James D. Miller. 2009. "Protecting the Integrity of the Polling Place: A Constitutional Defense of Poll Watcher Statutes." *Harvard Journal on Legislation*, 217: 217–242.

Herrnson, Paul, Richard Niemi, Michael Hamner, Peter Francia, Benjamin Bederson, Frederick Conrad, and Michael Traugott. 2008a. "Voter Reactions to Electronic Voting Systems: Results from a Usability Field Test." *American Politics Research*, 36: 580–611.

Herrnson, Paul, Richard G. Niemi, Michael J. Hanmer, Benjamin B. Bederson, Frederick G. Conrad, and Michael W. Traugott. 2008b. *Voting Technology: The Not-So-Simple Act of Casting a Ballot.* Washington, DC: Brookings Institution Press.

Herron, Michael C., and Jasjeet S. Sekhon. 2003. "Overvoting and Representation: An Examination of Overvoted Presidential Ballots in Broward and Miami-Dade Counties." *Electoral Studies*, 22: 21–47.

Herron, Michael C., and Jasjeet S. Sekhon. 2005. "Black Candidates and Black Voters: Assessing the Impact of Candidate Race on Uncounted Vote Rates." *Journal of Politics*, 67(1): 154–177.

Herron, Michael C., and Jonathan Wand. 2007. "Assessing Partisan Bias in Voting Technology: The Case of the 2004 New Hampshire Recount." *Electoral Studies*, 26(2): 247–261.

Hyde, Susan. (2008). "How International Election Observers Detect and Deter Fraud." In *Election Fraud: Detecting and Deterring Electoral Manipulation*, ed. R. Michael Alvarez, Thad E. Hall, and Susan Hyde. Washington, DC: Brookings Institution Press.

Hyde, Susan. 2010. "Experimenting in Democracy Promotion: International Observers and the 2004 Presidential Elections in Indonesia." *Perspectives on Politics*, 8: 511–527.

Internet Policy Institute. 2001. "Report of the National Workshop on Internet Voting. March 2001." http://www.internetpolicy.org/research/results.html.

Jamieson, Amie, Hyon B. Shin, and Jennifer Day. 2002. "Voting and Registration in the Election of November 2000." Current Population Reports, Series P-20, No. 542. Washington, DC: U.S. Bureau of the Census.

Karlan, Pamela, and Daniel R. Ortiz. 2002. "Congressional Authority to Regulate Elections." In *To Assure Pride and Confidence in the Electoral Process: Report of the National Commission on Federal Election Reform*. Washington, DC: Brookings Institution Press.

Keating, Dan. 2002. "Democracy Counts: The Media Consortium Florida Ballot Project." Paper presented at the 98th annual meeting of the American Political Science Association, Boston, MA.

Kelly, Janet M. 2005. "The Dilemma of the Unsatisfied Customer in a Market Model of Public Administration." *Public Administration Review*, 65: 76–84.

Kettl, Donald F. 1998. *Reinventing Government: A Fifth Year Report Card*. Washington, DC: Brookings Institution Press.

Kiewiet, D. Roderick, Thad E. Hall, R. Michael Alvarez, and Jonathan Katz. 2008. "Fraud or Failure? What Incident Reports Reveal about Election Anomalies and Irregularities." In *Election Fraud: Detecting and Deterring Electoral Manipulation*, ed. R. Michael Alvarez, Thad E. Hall, and Susan Hyde. Washington, DC: Brookings Institution Press.

Kimball, David C., and Brady Baybeck. 2008. "The Political Geography of Provisional Ballots." Paper presented at the American Political Science Association, Boston, MA.

Kimball, David C., and Martha Kropf. 2005. "Ballot Design and Unrecorded Votes on Paper-Based Ballots." *Public Opinion Quarterly*, 69(4): 508–529.

Kimball, David C., and Martha Kropf. 2008. "Voting Technology, Ballot Measures, and Residual Votes." *American Politics Research*, 36: 479–509.

Knack, Stephen, and Martha Kropf. 2001. "Who Uses Inferior Voting Technology?" Paper presented at the 2001 Public Choice Society Meeting, San Antonio, TX.

Knack, Stephen, and Martha Kropf. 2003a. "Voided Ballots in the 1996 Presidential Election: A County-Level Analysis." *Journal of Politics*, 65: 881–897.

Knack, Stephen, and Martha Kropf. 2003b. "Roll-Off at the Top of the Ballot: Intentional Undervoting in American Presidential Elections."*Politics and Policy*, 31: 575–594.

Kohno, Tadayoshi, Adam Stubblefield, Aviel D. Rubin, and Dan S. Wallach. 2004. "Analysis of an Electronic Voting System." In *Proceedings of the 2004 IEEE Symposium on Security and Privacy (S&P'04)*. DOI 10.1109/SECPRI.2004.1301313.

Levin, Ines, Gabe A. Cohn, Peter C. Ordeshook, and R. Michael Alvarez. 2009. "Detecting Voter Fraud in an Electronic Voting Context: An Analysis of the Unlimited Reelection Vote in Venezuela." Paper presented at the 2009 Electronic Voting Technology Workshop/Workshop on Trustworthy Elections, Montreal, Canada.

Magleby, David B., J. Quin Monson, and Kelly D. Patterson. 2007. *Dancing without Partners: How Candidates, Parties, and Interest Groups Interact in the Presidential Campaign*. Lanham, MD: Rowman and Littlefield.

Mebane, Walter R., Jr. 2004. "The Wrong Man Is President! Overvotes in the 2000 Presidential Election in Florida." *Perspectives on Politics*, 2: 525–535.

Mebane, Walter R., Jr. 2010. "Election Fraud or Strategic Voting? Can Second-digit Tests Tell the Difference?" Prepared for presentation at the 2010 Summer Meeting of the Political Methodology Society, University of Iowa, July 22–24, 2010.

Moynihan, Donald P. 2006. "Managing for Results in State Government: Evaluating a Decade of Reform." *Public Administration Review*, 66: 77–89.

Moynihan, Donald P. 2008. *The Dynamics of Performance Management: Constructing Information and Reform*. Washington, DC: Georgetown University Press.

Myagkov, Mikhail, Peter C. Ordeshook, and Dimitri Shakin. 2008. *The Forensics of Election Fraud: Russia and Ukraine*. New York: Cambridge University Press.

Norden, Lawrence, Jeremy Creeland, Ana Munoz, and W. Quesenbery. 2006. *The Machinery of Democracy: Protecting Elections in an Electronic World*. New York: Brennan Center Justice, NYU Law School.

Odegaard, David. 2009. "Behavior and Error in Election Administration: A Look at Election Day Precinct Reports." University of New Mexico.

O'Toole, Laurence J., Jr., and Kenneth J. Meier. 1999. "Modeling the Impact of Public Management: Implications of Structural Context." *Journal of Public Administration Research and Theory*, 9(4): 505–526.

O'Toole, Laurence J., Jr., and Kenneth J. Meier. 2003. "Bureaucracy and Uncertainty."In *Uncertainty in American Politics*, ed. Barry Burden. Cambridge: Cambridge University Press.

Pastor, Robert A. 1998. "Mediating Elections." *Journal of Democracy*, 9(1): 154–163.

Rainey, Hal G., and Paula Steinbauer. 1999."Galloping Elephants: Developing Elements of a Theory of Effective Government Organizations." *Journal of Public Administration Research and Theory.* (9), 1: 1–32.

Rosenstone, Steven, and John Mark Hansen. 1993. *Mobilization, Participation, and American Democracy.* New York: Macmillan.

Rosenstone, Steven, and Raymond Wolfinger. 1978. "The Effect of Registration Laws on Voter Turnout." *American Political Science Review*, 72: 22–45.

Simpser, Alberto. 2008. "The Unintended Consequences of Election Monitoring." In *Election Fraud: Detecting and Deterring Electoral Manipulation*, ed. R. Michael Alvarez, Thad Hall, and Susan Hyde. Washington, DC: Brookings Institution Press.

Sinclair, Betsy, and R. Michael Alvarez. 2004. "Who Overvotes, Who Undervotes, Using Punchcards? Evidence from Los Angeles County." *Political Research Quarterly*, 57(1): 15–25.

Singleton, Royce, Jr., Bruce Straits, Margaret Straits, and R. J. McAllister. 1988. *Approaches to Social Research.* New York: Oxford University Press.

Stein, Robert, Greg Vonnahme, Michael Byrne, and Daniel Wallach. 2008. "Voting Technology, Election Administration, and Voter Performance." *Election Law Journal: Rules, Politics, and Policy*, 7: 123–135.

Stewart, Charles, III. 2004. "The Reliability of Electronic Voting Machines in Georgia." Working Paper 20, Caltech/MIT Voting Technology Project.

Stewart, Charles, III. 2006. "Residual Vote in the 2004 Election." *Election Law Journal: Rules, Politics, and Policy*, 5(2): 158–169.

Tomz, Michael, and Robert P. van Houweling. 2003. "How Does Voting Equipment Affect the Racial Gap in Voided Ballots?" *American Journal of Political Science*, 47(1): 46–60.

Truscott, William. 2003. *Six Sigma: Continual Improvement for Business.* Waltham, MA: Butterworth-Heinemann.

Wand, Jonathan, Kenneth Shotts, Walter R. Mebane, Jasjeet S. Sekhon, Michael Herron, and Henry E. Brady. 2001. "The Butterfly Did It: The Aberrant Vote for Buchanan in Palm Beach County, Florida." *American Political Science Review*, 95(4): 793–810.

Webb, Eugene, Donald Campbell, Richard Schwartz, and Lee Sechrest. 1966. *Unobtrusive Measures: Nonreactive Research in the Social Sciences.* Chicago, IL: RAND.

Wolter, Kirk, Diana Jergovic, Whitney Moore, Joe Murphy, and Colm O'Muircheartaigh. 2003. "Reliability of the Uncertified Ballots in the 2000 Presidential Election in Florida." *American Statistician*, 57(1): 1–14.

Index